LEGENDS OF THE RED RIVER VALLEY

"Just a minute, brother, before you go on with your lambastin'. Is that th' Skillet over yonder?" asked the ex-lieutenant of the Rangers.
"Yep, that's hit. Ye want hit?" answered the driver.

LEGENDS OF THE RED RIVER VALLEY

- BY -

BRIGHT RAY

ILLUSTRATIONS BY
FRANK ANTHONY STANUSH

COMMONWEALTH BOOK COMPANY

Copyright © 1941 by The Naylor Company
Copyright © 2023 by Commonwealth Book Company, Inc.

All rights reserved. No part of this book may be reproduced in any form or by any means without the prior written consent of the publisher, excepting brief quotes used in reviews.
Printed in the United States of America.

ISBN: 978-1-948986-52-6

CONTENTS

	PAGE
1 Vignettes of the Tejas	1
2 A Champagne Supper in the Valley . . .	17
3 When Shelby Passed This Way	26
4 Plain and Fancy Riding	36
5 Soldiers in the Cellar	45
6 Mystery of Black Hollow	68
7 Kentuckians' Rendezvous	81
8 Legend of Caddo Lake	92
9 Paris Fantasy	100
10 Exploits of Andy Thomas	111
11 Pioneer Child	126
12 A Path Through the Sand	139

13
Quantrell, Guerrilla Chieftain 147
14
The Lady Isabella 156
15
Lick Skillet Men 167
16
"On the Banks of the Washita" 181
17
The House of the Screaming Peacocks . . 191
18
Loom of Destiny 200
19
"As Long as Water Runs" 214
20
Men of Mystery 223
21
Aunt Maria Speaks Her Mind 231
22
Remembrance 240
23
Lost Colleges 242
24
Sidelight on a Robber 244
25
The Snake Editor Speaks 247
26
When the Railroads Came to the Valley . . 253

FOREWORD

On a red-leaved day in mid-October I stood in a crowded, glass-enclosed observation platform overlooking Red River and watched machines shoveling dirt, transferring sand from one side of the river to the other, moulding huge conduits into shape, blasting trees from their hitherto secure foundations and leveling hills that had sheltered the buffalo, the Indian and the white man. Situated on a high bluff (which the machines had as yet not decided to move), the platform afforded us box seats for a drama that was breath-taking in its vastness. Probably none of us there that day grasped its full comprehension; we were only sight-seers out to watch the construction of a dam—a Government dam that was to protect Memphis and New Orleans from Father Mississippi's old tricks and to furnish cheap electricity to dwellers in the Red River Valley.

The sunshine was brilliant that day and visibility was unlimited. Upstream the horizon touched Preston Bend. Beyond that, I knew, were old Red River Station and Doan's Crossing; downstream were Bonham, Paris and the flats of East Texas. Across stream was Oklahoma with a Governor opposing the disturbance of the river bed and its adjacent plains; Boggy Depot's ruins were over there somewhere near, and so was old Fort Washita, the rendezvous of Federals, Confederates and Indians.

Seventy-five years ago men had made their way back here from a war, tired, hungry and penniless. They drove their cattle and wagons across the river at Baer's Ferry, Colbert's Ferry and Rock Bluff Ferry. They began a new chapter in the river's history and predicted that commerce and industry would cross at the same spots where they pushed their cattle down the banks.

The scene from our observation platform indicated the truth of their prediction. I stood on the exact spot of Baer's Ferry and watched a young man finishing the details of a working model of the dam. Now and then my eyes turned outward to the river where the fifty-million-dollar project was taking actual form. The drama of its construction held me in wonder.

I found myself wondering too about the river's past, its part in the settlement of the valley. I resolved to search for the forgotten first chapters of the river's story. My quest led me far and I found many stories. Some of them were moulded, faded and moth-eaten; some stirring and vigorous; some tender and pathetic; some gay and boisterous.

I pass these legends on to you. Perhaps they make the story of any great river that after many years of mastery is being harnessed with machines and forced to produce and protect where formerly it threatened and persecuted. Our rivers are being tamed for the very thing they used to flaunt—their power.

—*The Author*

— VIGNETTES OF THE TEJAS —

I

Spring had come again to the land of the Tejas. The streams were filled with fish; the corn was high and the grass was green. The call of the chase was strong and the buffalo challenged the skill of the hunter.

Beside the banks of the Neches an Indian brave stood watching a flaming sunset. It was the eve of the spring buffalo hunt; on the calendar of the white man it was the year of our Lord 1515. Nashihoto, strongest and bravest of the sons of the chief, had stolen away from the council fire to stand by the river's edge and dream. The yellow of the sunset melted into the blue of evening. The first bright star appeared. Far down the stream a canoe with a lone occupant was outlined clearly in the twilight dusk. Motionless, with arms crossed and eyes half-closed, the young chieftain watched the canoe disappear. The evening star brightened and Nashihoto found himself thinking of his tribe; of the peaceful village which lay back of him; of the corn and melon patches now thriving in the spring weather; of the green grass and of the coming hunt. At dawn the warriors would ride forth on the buffalo hunt. Far to the south, as far as the Great River, would they ride.

Nashihoto stood long in his dreams to allow the peaceful solitude to fill his being. He was proud that he was a chieftain of the Tejas, a tribe that loved peace and domesticity. No other tribe had such fine fields of corn and melons; no other tribe had such villages and no other tribe had such good hunters. Nashihoto had roamed the forests and the plains from the Naugdoches* on the north to the Great River on the south. Some day he would rule the Tejas; not only the Tejas, he was thinking, but a vast country of the Caddos, the Wacos, the Nassonites and the Orquinzacos. All would be subject to Nashihoto. Like the star which now sparkled in the west, so the Tejas should shine among the other tribes; like the lone canoe forging ahead down the river the Tejas should lead the way for others to follow. So deep in thought was he that he did not hear a stealthy step beside him.

"Nashihoto, the chief desires thee—" It was Star-Eyes, the loveliest Indian maiden of the village, who had followed him. Did not her eyes always follow him? Did she not know how he liked to steal away in solitude when other warriors sat around the teepees and the

---

* Naugdoches—The Red (on Spanish maps)—from name of Indian tribe.

campfires? Did she not long for one word from him?

"Ah, beautiful one, stars of the sky are not brighter than eyes of Star-Eyes. Through both I see great land of the Tejas. Through many moons, in seasons yet to come, this land from the Naugdoches to the Great River shall be called the land of the Tejas. Be it so; come, let us return to the chieftain's fire."

II

It was April, 1687; seated on a pine log before a crude little hut was a Chevalier of France and his trusted body-guard. The hour was sunset and the Chevalier's eyes were fixed upon the bright colors of the sky reflected in the waters of the Arkakisa while those of his companion were set upon the careful study of a map. The Chevalier turned and spoke.

"*Mon ami*, what dost thou find upon the map?"

"Ah, monsieur, I am but studying our location and endeavoring to mark it."

"*C'est bien*, Joutel; Chief Nashihoto of the friendly Indians in yon village calls this stream the Arkakisa* but we shall call it the River of Canoes since we had to borrow so many to cross it."

"*Oui*, monsieur, truly; we have come a long

---

* Arkakisa—Indian for the Trinity.

way since we crossed the River of Beeves* and even the River of Canes** is now some distance away."

"This land of the Tejas is a mighty land, mon Joutel. Such rivers and such forests! It will add much to the glory of *La Belle France* and her sovereign."

Joutel was silent as he traced the records that in after years proved priceless. The Chevalier La Salle picked up his sword and looked long at the fleur-de-lis engraved upon its hilt. "*Mais oui*, Joutel, the lilies of France shall not be vanquished! I am determined that we shall reach the fort of my faithful De Tonti. There we shall rest at the new settlement before we plunge on to find what you call the fatal river of De Soto."

Dusk deepened. Soft sounds of cautious steps broke the silence. Father Antoine, the priest, appeared.

"My son," he said quietly to the Chevalier, "there are serious matters to discuss with thee. I know the trusty Joutel here and am not afraid to speak before him. I must tell you that there is discontent in our little company and I fear for thy safety."

"Father Antoine, you pay too much attention to the whisperings of the men. We shall yet find trace of Moragnet and Nika. All will be well; this is New France. Come, let us walk

---

* River of Beeves—The Lavaca.
** River of Canes—The Colorado.

toward the sunset and talk these worries of thine into nothings. *A bientot,* Joutel."

Nemesis followed them upon that fateful evening. The fears of the good father Antoine had been well-founded, for treason was running riot in the small band of explorers. Death, dangers and desertions had played havoc with the Chevalier's idealistic plan of colonization. Jealousy and envy were uppermost in the hearts of the two skulking figures who watched the commander's evening stroll. From behind the pine trees near the river's edge they bided the moment of destruction. The sunset faded; flaming colors gave way to deep purples.

"My son, thou must be careful in what thou sayest about—"

A sudden shot pierced the evening's stillness. "Too late, Father," answered the gallant Chevalier as he fell back into the arms of the priest. "Thy warning comes too late. I should have listened to thee sooner but it was for my country—and my king. Someday—the fleur-de-lis——"

The April night closed in upon them. The cry of the mourning dove rose above the sighing of the pines as the faithful priest paid the last tribute to a favorite of Louis XIV. Strange grave for the Chevalier La Salle, friend of the Grand Monarch, here in the Indian country beside the newly-marked River of Canoes! Father Antoine prayed silently and long at his task while a map-maker put away his maps saying, "Darkness prevents my writing but I must guard well these records for *La Belle France*. Someday she may need them."

But such a day was far distant—as distant as the stars and as unknown. So said Chief Nashihoto to his braves sitting in council with him that night in the Tejas village. The big strong paleface and his braves had left strange and beautiful gifts and had taken canoes to cross the river. But paleface would learn soon this was Tejas' land. Chief Nashihoto left the campfire and walked to the river's edge. He looked upward through the tall pines to the stars—he listened contentedly to the familiar sound of the mourning dove. Tejas' land as long as grass grew and water ran.

III

Near dusk on an April evening in 1719 a lone Indian rider approached the mission of San Antonio de Valero in the village of Bexar. He stopped near the gates and slid from his pony to listen. He heard, faintly, the chanting of the monks at their evening prayers. He remembered other nights and other days when he had stood at the side of the good fathers to listen. Then he had been a boy touched by the story they told him. Now he was a brave of the Tejas, successor to the chieftain who had told him that these fathers at the mission—and their warriors who would follow them—had come to take the hunting ground of the red man.

The mission bells sounded the hour of seven. Father Sebastian came to close and lock the outer gates. He stood for a moment gazing at the red horizon and thinking in his heart a prayer for this new land. So fervent was his prayer that it became audible. "This New Spain shall be a marvelous and mighty land."

Out of the dusk a soft voice, clear and cool as the patio fountain, answered him. "New Spain this shall never be, Father. This is Tejas' land. For countless ages her warriors have hunted on its prairies and taken fish from its streams. True, you have given us much. From the books in your mission I have learned how other men live across the sea but you have not taught me that this land shall ever be yours."

Father Sebastian had stepped back in surprise but at the sound of this soft voice he smiled kindly. "Ah, Nashihoto, what brings you here? At first you alarmed me by speaking from nowhere and now you speak with strange ideas. What has happened to you in the six months since you left the mission?"

"All day I have been riding to see again these friendly walls and to hear your voice. Likely I come no more, Father. I have been in the camps of the Tejas, the Caddos, the Wacos; all beat the war drums. Take warning, Father; this land you call New Spain has long been theirs. The stars tell them it always will be."

He vanished into the dusk as noiselessly as he had come. Father Sebastian turned the lock but stood a moment at the mission gates gazing upward through the poplar leaves at the glistening stars overhead.

"Ah, well, who knows? Who has ever known what the stars foretell? Shall we be able to keep this mighty country for the Holy Father at Rome, or shall the red man regain his own? Or neither? Only the All-Wise knows the answer."

The bells chimed the passing of another hour. Father Sebastian retraced his steps. Darkness enclosed the mission of San Antonio de Valero.

IV

In the early summer of 1821 the century-old San Antonio, now the provisional capital of Texas, was ablaze with tropical bloom and color. Above the Palace of the Governors where the flag of Spain had long been seen, floated the flag of a new republic—the bright red, green and white of Mexico.

Toward noon of this June day four men, equally distinguished in appearance, made their way across Military Plaza to the Governors' Palace. The plaza was crowded with traders and merchants, and the two genial men who led the party were constantly being stopped with cries of *"Buenos dias,* Señor Veramendi; *gracias,* Señor Seguin." Many turned to watch the two strangers with them—a tall, handsome American from the States, and an Indian, slender and sinewy, who wore the dress of a hunter and evidently was the friend and guide of the young American.

Upon reaching the palace they were quickly admitted into the room where the Governor rose from his chair behind a great table to greet them cordially. "Ah, Señor Veramendi, you are prompt. I see that you and Señor Seguin have brought with you the traveler of whom we have heard so much."

"Yes, your excellency; may we have the pleasure of presenting to you the young friend of Baron de Bastrop, Señor Stephen F. Austin and his friend, Chief Nashihoto of the Tejas?"

"Ah, Señor, you are both welcome to San Antonio. We have expected you. You wish, I believe, to carry out the plans of your father and bring colonists to this province."

"Yes, your excellency, such is my desire."

"The republic of Mexico is friendly to this enterprise. Who knows but what that flag that you were gazing at so intently a moment ago may one day be the flag of a whole continent? Señor Austin, you are to select land along the Colorado and the Brazos for your colonization grant."

"Thanks, your excellency; I desire to help the province and I pledge my every effort to the carrying out of my father's plan. With your kind permission and the help of Chief Nashihoto here I shall set out at once."

"One moment, Señor Austin; before you go let us show you the maps. Be seated, gentlemen." The Indian remained silent and stationary. "You, too, Chief, you are to guide this gentleman and El Colorado may lead you far—"

Nashihoto disdainfully approached the table. "No need paper—go Indian way."

Nevertheless, it was an hour before Austin said good-bye to Veramendi and Seguin and walked slowly across the plaza. His mind was whirling with the cordiality of his reception, and the hospitality of his Spanish friends. He wanted time to think. He paused and looked back at the palace.

"Nashihoto, what do men here think of his Excellency, the Governor?"

Nashihoto remained impassive and answered slowly: "His Excellency thinks only of Mexico; mistreat Indian and white man alike. He sees only the flag above his house."

"While you, Nashihoto, what do *you* see?"

"I see flag torn down—forgotten. This land, white man, belong to *my* people—to Tejas— to Caddos and Wacos—to all tribes that live upon its prairies or hunt upon its hills. It is Indian's hunting-ground; I know—my father say so—his father say same to him. You white man but you my friend."

"Yes, Nashihoto, I know what you mean. I agree with you to some extent. I too see that flag torn down, but I see a new flag in its place."

The crowds in the plaza hid them from view. The sultriness and heat of early afternoon foretold *siesta* time for all. So the builder of the

VIGNETTES OF THE TEJAS

future and the dreamer of the past hastened their steps toward Señor Veramendi's home. The image of Mexico's flag was fixed in the memory of Stephen F. Austin and the vision of another was hardly less clear.

V

On the 22nd of October, 1836, there was much excitement in the little town of Columbia-on-the-Brazos. Above the roof of a small wooden building there floated the flag of a new republic with its colors of red, white and blue encircling a single star. On this day General Sam Houston was to be inaugurated as President of Texas.

"What will he do about Santa Anna?" whispered the populace. "Maybe another Mexican mystery ship will slip into the Brazos and this time succeed in getting away," or "Better increase the guard around the prisoner than to give him his freedom"; some were even heard to say "Watch the President or he'll let Santa Anna get away."

For six months the fate of Santa Anna had been hanging in the balance of political turmoil. The unsuccessful attempt of the Passaic to steal the prisoner had not been forgotten. All other schemes of escape had been thwarted, but many were fearful that the President would show mercy to one they felt should have no mercy.

The hum of talk grew quieter; the time of the inauguration ceremony approached. In the crowd that milled around the temporary capitol one figure stood alone on the steps, silent and stationary.

"That's one of the Gen'r'l's Indian friends over there," said one onlooker to another. Then he added with a sly look, "You know he's had plenty o' Indian friends, one sort an' another. This here one claims he's a chief of th' old Tejas tribe; what's left of it. Taken quite a fancy to th' Gen'r'l and thinks he's helpin' rule th' land."

"Well, he's a stout fellow, I can see, and I wouldn't want him for my enemy. But sure as shootin', there's the Gen'r'l ridin' up. Push on in there."

The commanding figure of Sam Houston shrank all others into a solid mass that surrounded him, as he took the oath of office. Later there was tremendous cheering as the soldier-hero unbuckled his sword with the remark "This is the emblem of my past office. I expect to resume it if the danger of my country needs it."

He finally broke through the mass and stopped to speak to a silent figure in the doorway. "Come on, Nashihoto; let us get out of this and into the open."

He made his way briskly to the hitching rack. His Indian friend followed noiselessly. "Well, Nashihoto, how do you like our little flag with the lone star?" he asked as he looked back at the building. "We call it the star of freedom; I hope it may be just that. And the first step I intend to take is to release General Santa Anna. A prisoner of war shall be so treated; let the people think what they may."

The Indian still gazed at the flag above the capitol. "Excellency, you have been my friend of the trail but I think your new flag does not mean freedom for all. My father say this would be Indian's country as long as grass grew and water ran. That lone star there is the white man's sign."

Later that day when the President reached the quiet of his simple quarters he pondered the words of Nashihoto and the fate of Santa Anna. Then he reached for pen and paper. The freedom of the Lone Star should soon be tried; and if occasion demanded, it should be tested.

VI

Nearly twenty-five years passed by. It was dusk of a February afternoon in 1861. President Houston was now Governor Houston. The city of Austin, capital of the Lone Star State, was seething with excitement. People were found at every street corner and in every public place with the one topic *secession* cementing their talk into delirious unity.

Governor Houston had withdrawn from the crowds and sat alone in his study, gazing thoughtfully into the log fire. Alone, that is, except for a solitary figure by the window. Nashihoto, the Indian, was still his friend.

Governor Houston's sentiments against secession were considered absurd by many groups of Austin people that night; in fact, the whole state had turned against him and disregarded his plea for unity within the Union. Hot-headed youth had refused to listen to the wisdom of age. A Special Convention was in session without the Governor's orders, consent, or desire. It had that day voted to dissolve the union with the United States and join the Confederacy. Furthermore, it had voted uproariously for a resolution declaring the office of Governor to be vacant.

The erst-while Governor sighed and glanced toward the window. "Nashihoto, I am weary. I long for the peace of the Indian village."

"Excellency, have I not always said this is Indian's country?" He came across and leaned lightly on the mantel.

"Yes, *I* know, Nashihoto, but my people do not know that. It seems they do not know what they want. Twenty-five years ago they made the new flag of the one star; then for fifteen years they have cheered the Stars and Stripes. Now they would change again, to the Stars and Bars."

"Too much talk about stars; all same to me. Only first stars should count and that is Indian's star in sky."

Houston rose and walked to the window. He looked beyond the city of Austin to the hills of the Colorado. "My friend, let us hope that the Great Spirit that rules these hills and stars will lead my people through the troublous times ahead."

The sound of bells came to them followed by the discord of happy, excited voices. The two figures in the Governor's office were silent. The Indian was oblivious of both sound and scene; he was the last of his race and he was dreaming of a forgotten legend of the Tejas, but the Governor listened with a heavy heart.

VII

"Inauguration Day" in Austin in the late 1930's was an epochal occasion. Brilliant sunshine flooded the city and changed the chromium trimmings of the Municipal Building to glaring silver streaks; it hung upon the capitol dome from whence it radiated blistering rays of heat and finally it settled upon a football stadium with sun-tanning intensity. The six multi-colored flags of Texas lined Congress Avenue and the streets to the stadium to make the entire city a splash of color.

Austin was crowded. Ranchmen from the plains rubbed shoulders with cotton farmers from the bottom lands. Oil men from the east and south overflowed upon the scene. Traffic officers and State Police shunted cars about with the dexterity and the methods of the cowpunchers driving cattle in "th' ol' corral."

University students and candid camera fiends climbed up and down and over a temporary stage erected at the football stadium where later on a historical pageant was to be presented. Performers in costumes of pioneers, Mexicans, Frenchmen, Indians and Spaniards assembled in the bedlam.

It was only a masquerade, but in the group costumed as Indians there was one who had real Indian blood in his veins. He came from the valley of the Red River in Oklahoma and none of his confreres knew he was 'part Indian.' He was deeply stirred by the role he was enacting. He imagined himself a descendant of that lost tribe of the Tejas, or the Caddos or the Wacos. His father was a white man and so was his grandfather. But further back there had been a chieftain whom his grandmother had described many times. Could it have been that Nashitoto who so long ago had dreamed of a Tejas Empire?

When the pageant had ended and twenty-one guns had proclaimed the reign of a new governor, people scattered to many points to celebrate. Verily, a great empire had been established here; a thriving and united state looked forward. But it was the white man's empire; it was the answer to Houston's prayer. His people had come through troublous times and faced prosperity.

The Tejas played well his part; the empire bears his name.

Brownie seemed to sense the urgency of the situation. Intuitively he felt his mistress' needs and he responded gratefully with speed and accuracy. He cleared the picket fence of the lot before his would-be captors realized the white 'boy's' trick.

2

—A CHAMPAGNE SUPPER IN THE VALLEY—

There is a stirring story of the Butterfield Trail which has to do with a champagne supper and a courthouse. The Butterfield Trail was the fast overland Express from Saint Louis to San Francisco. It was the American Airlines of the 1850's and its promoter and owner, Colonel George P. Butterfield, was feted and toasted wherever he made his appearance. Every luxury that it was possible to obtain was provided for the passengers of his line. Your ticket at Saint Louis cost you $200 whereupon you settled yourself for a comfortable ride of 2795 miles in a period of 21 days.

The Trail led southward through Arkansas and the Indian Territory and crossed Red River at Colbert's Ferry. It was hailed as the world's longest stage route and had a mileage in Texas alone of 767 miles. Passengers often began to think that Texas extended from Red River to the Pacific. Stops were made every ten or twenty miles and these stage-stands were very well kept and luxurious, not at all bad predecessors of the compact filling-stations of today. Horses were changed at each stop so that the speed of seven miles an hour could be maintained. Speed was essential in those days, and Col. Butterfield overlooked no detail in that regard. There was always a good eating house at each stand and also stables and blacksmiths' shops. Overnight stops were made at commodious inns.

Colonel Butterfield's main obligation was to get the mail through to the west coast. He had secured a contract from the Government for six years at a yearly salary of $600,000. Each of his coaches carried passengers—sometimes six, sometimes ten—who made up an extra dividend for Colonel Butterfield and his associates. Somehow business men found out early in our history that the way to get a business going in this country was to get a good government contract.

The Butterfield Coach Lines furnished the latest models in coaches—the Stream-Liners of the Fifties had Concord springs, and plush upholstery. Sleek, well-fed horses were used until they reached Texas. At Fort Belknap it was customary to change to the wiry Spanish, or Texas mules. This was done as a precautionary measure since the Kiowa Indians who constituted the Highway Patrol of that time, cared not a feather-weight for mules whereas horses were usually impounded immediately for private use.

The last big station in the Indian Territory was at Boggy Depot, fifteen or twenty miles north of Red River. Colbert's Ferry crossing was used for the entrance into Texas, and at

A CHAMPAGNE SUPPER

Sherman, county seat of Grayson County and ten or fifteen miles from the ferry, the Company built a large and commodious station. Mail for the Red River Valley was deposited here and mail for the west coast was picked up. Twice a week the stage came through and stopped for overnight. It was a long rough ride from Boggy Depot and passengers were more than glad to rest at what looked like the beginnings of civilization. But by the time they reached Fort Belknap and saw the Texas mules as their means of transportation they probably thought they had been badly fooled at the town near Red River.

Sherman was an up-and-coming town then; it appreciated Colonel Butterfield and the business he brought with his coaches. It knew all about the $50,000 bet he made with a steamship company that he could beat their best boat to San Francisco and side bets were placed freely by its citizens that the Overland Mail would beat the boat. Not only Sherman but the whole country knew about the wager; from coast to coast bets were laid and all without the aid of the columnists and commentators of the press, the radio or the films.

Colonel Butterfield won his wager, beating his own record and making the trip to San Francisco in 21 days flat. All Texans said it was due to the speed and endurance of the Texas mules in the 767 miles across Texas. Citizens of the Red River country had more champagne and Madeira wine than has been known in the country since. Whether it came in by the Butterfield coaches or by private conveyance from the port of Jefferson or by wagon, carriage and ox-cart from the old country mattered not; it got there. It is not surprising therefore that the citizens of the county seat of Grayson County honored Colonel Butterfield and some of his associates with a champagne supper. The legend runs that this pre-Rotary, ante-Chamber-of-Commerce banquet was staged as a gesture of esteem for his services in developing Texas, and bringing trade, tourists and settlers.

The sponsors were very frank about labeling the affair—a "champagne supper." The supper was given in the dining-room of the Company's eating-house and of course was inaugurated by drinking several champagne toasts. Thereafter, although there were such delicacies as wild turkey, venison, and buffalo steak, the champagne flavor was added to everything. There was good music for the occasion too; in 1858 it was a very simple matter to get an orchestra, price or expense not to be considered. The message was sent around to the slave-owners to send their best darkies to play for the supper. From all around they came—Colbert's Ferry, Pilot Grove, Baer's Ferry, Preston, Glen Eden, Warren, Bonham and Sherman. The players—on this occasion about fifteen or twenty—appeared with their fiddles, their banjos, their guitars and mandolins; all filled with excitement and glee for the privilege of playing at a big supper. It was an all-string orchestra of course and it

A CHAMPAGNE SUPPER

gave out a plaintive, wailing, tickling mood that would rival the hypnotic wailing of any Hawaiian Room today. The boys spent no time in practices and rehearsals for that would have been a waste of their owners' time; the fiddler set the tune and the tempo and the rest joined in when they felt like it, usually about the fourth beat. Deeds of prowess and endurance were re-told, all dealing with the white man's victory over the Indian; mules, buffaloes and cows were extolled for their sundry and various qualities.

"Your mail-coach would a' never got to San Francisco, Colonel Butterfield, if it hadn' a' been for our Texas mules. Th' Indians don't like 'em; wouldn' have 'em, but they put you through Texas."

"Ain't nothin' like a good buffalo steak such as you git here in North Texas. Finest meat in th' world."

"Ceptin' venison. I'll hunt deer 'stid o' buffalo any day, even if you do git more fer th' hides. Ain't no trouble to git a deer here, any day."

"I'll take wild turkey fer mine; they're so plentiful roun' here I can shoot five at a time when I sight a covey."

"Drivin' these here cows and calves to Kansas is th' hope o' this country. If we can jus' git 'em to Abilene why we can feed the whole world. They're ever'where; we jus got to round 'em up. Th' res' of th' world likes t' eat beef."

Bets were exchanged on what constituted the best eating, the best drinking and the best riding, and how much good was going to happen to the country because of Colonel Butterfield's 767 miles across Texas.

"This is goin' t' be th' biggest town in Texas, right here, Colonel. We got a courthouse and two hundred people already and more's comin' in all th' time."

"Yep, people and cows goin' t' stay in this country. Th' deer an' th' buffalo may go but th' people and th' cows gonna stay. Why, I'll bet ya' by all th' eggs in th' ol' gray goose's nest that we'll have 500 people here in ten years, an' Colonel Butterfield, you'll hep' t' do it."

"I'll take you up on that; all th' eggs in th' ol' gray goose's nest 'ginst my best buffalo skin a-hangin' in my smoke-house that we'll have 750 folks here."

"You can't do that; you can't bet them eggs 'cause you can't git t' them eggs. Th' ol' goose's done moved her nest under th' courthouse. S'fact, I been seein' her come out from under fer a week or more, so change yer stakes, gentlemen!"

"I ain't agreein' that she's moved but if she has who says I can't git her eggs? Th' bet stands; fill up th' glasses, boys. We'll git them eggs if we have to take th' courthouse down. All th' eggs 'ginst th' best buffalo skin in Bill Roberts' smoke-house."

More champagne was drunk while the colored boys with their banjos and their fiddles

A CHAMPAGNE SUPPER

kept playing their rollicking tunes to match the mood. There must have been few, if any women at the banquet. A dinner for fifty men demanded the assistance of women to the tavern keeper. They supervised the menu, they sent extra dishes and they directed the serving by the slaves. Those that did not get in on this committee were at home anxiously awaiting the story from their men-folks. There was only the grapevine telegraph system but in some cases it was known to surpass any other means of communication. The old gray goose was likely a very familiar figure around the courthouse. Everybody seemed to know her. It was said that she always made her nest in the southeast corner of the courthouse yard.

"He's goin' t' hunt th' ol' gray goose's nest," flashed the message over the invisible-non-existent wires of the g-v-t.

"We'll git them eggs. Bill's done made his bet an' if we shoot th' buffalo here tonight we got t' git them stakes here."

The last statement led to a general exodus from the banquet-hall. Diners, waiters, supervisors, slaves and musicians moved out to hunt the goose's eggs. The champagne moved with them. The supervisors and the slaves saw to that. There was a war-like ring to the statement that drove them from the doors of the tavern. "Shoot the Buffalo" and "Git th' stakes" was no fighting slogan or battle cry; on the contrary it was a social diversion. "Shoot the Buffalo" was a good, lively square dance which all the people attended. It probably derived its name from the excitement following a buffalo hunt. At any rate it was enjoyable and perfectly permissible for women and children. On this warm, balmy evening in early fall when the company reached the courthouse yard the colored boys went right on with their rollicking music and the slaves served the champagne from a barrel under the trees. The bettors chose sides for the attack on the courthouse.

What a night it was! Plank by plank they went at the quest of the goose's nest. When early dawn came there was nothing left of the courthouse; but the men had found the eggs of the old gray goose. The two attacking parties agreed that the old gray goose had really moved her nest without notification being filed and she had moved so far underneath that the entire house had to be taken down before her nest was found. Weary but happy men counted the eggs and turned them over to a fellow-member designated to hold the stakes. They then moved on en masse, which meant that they dragged the Colonel of the Stagelines, willy-nilly, to get the buffalo skin from Bill Roberts' smoke-house. The sleepy colored boys followed with their fiddles and their music but the champagne barrel was dry. They had long since forgotten what the bet was; they only remembered the stakes.

There was just one thing that bothered the Sheriff when he returned to open the courthouse. He had a notice of sale and his orders said to post it on the courthouse door, but there was no courthouse and no door. The conviviality and the ingenious wit of the night before with its flowing champagne flavor must have remained with him and prompted his solution of the problem. He poked around the ruins and found a door, which he immediately picked up and propped against a tree—fortunately they had not taken the trees down—tacked his notice of sale thereon and strolled merrily across the Square to look for further business of the day.

Oh well, what did it matter? The place was well-marked indeed, for today there stands a million-dollar courthouse of stone and concrete above the spot where the old gray goose once had her nest, and fifteen thousand people mill round it every day and admire it.

3

— WHEN SHELBY PASSED THIS WAY —

Bonham is about the oldest town in the valley. For a little over one hundred years it has been a trading-post for the people of the rich lowlands of the river. I had seen it many times but I had never seen it more resplendent than on a day in the fall of 1940 when it welcomed a figure of political prominence. The Speaker of the House of Representatives at Washington had come home for a brief recess. *Home* in his case was Bonham. Not often has Texas boasted such an honor as the Speakership of the National House. Of course, there was the little city of Uvalde, away off in the southcentral part of the state where a certain distinguished Cactus Jack lives. But this was Sam Rayburn, gentleman-farmer of Fannin County, the staunch friend and ally of the Red River Dam Project. In fact, the whole idea of the dam would have remained hidden in the cigarette smoke and pipe dreams of visionaries if it hadn't been for Sam. No wonder then that there were placards screaming—"Thank you Sam, for the Dam!" In the calmness of retrospection—had I been capable of such that day —I would have remembered that Cactus Jack himself was born in the Red River Valley, just a little farther eastward toward the sandy land; so was the President of the State University.

But this was Bonham, hovering between the black land and the red. The white stone courthouse erected in 1888 looked fresh and clean in the bright sunshine; it looked extremely well and its age sat lightly upon its cupola; so lightly that one heard no rumors of the necessity of a new courthouse. In these days of destruction, many counties find it effective to tear down old courthouses and build new, modern ones with the aid of loans from the Government; but not so here. All building-talk centered around the dam and its accruing business and profits.

The yard of the courthouse was crowded. River folks tramped carelessly over the green grass and flowers. Green trees above them still offered their shade although it was late October. Two sentries of the Square remained serene. At the southeast corner James Butler Bonham, in beautiful bronze, extended his hand in welcome, while on the northwest corner the Confederate soldier of granite stood guard with gun in hand to remind one that he had fought for "gallantry, daring and dash."

There was an inscription on the granite that told me this and there was a very old gentleman standing on the sidewalk near me that corroborated it. He was slender and active and there was a decided twinkle in his blue, blue eyes. Probably that twinkle was the remnant of the dash mentioned on the granite. He saw me reading the inscription and studying the figure while we waited for a parade which was forming in the outskirts of Main Street.

"Yep, I was one of *them;* one of them boys in gray and I joined up right here on *this* same Square; lots o' people here today, honey, jus' like it was th' day Shelby and his men passed through here. That's when I joined. I was jus' a kid of sixteen but when Shelby came through I went right on with him; so did a lot o' other boys. Shelby's Escort, that's what it was. See this pin here in my coat, honey? Look at it."

I looked at a loop of ribbon in his coat-lapel and recognized the small bronze decoration as a Maltese cross bestowed by the United Daughters of the Confederacy. The light in the old gentleman's eye indicated that the Cross of Honor was a matter of great pride to him. Was it for bravery in battle, I wondered. It was easy to think of battle for in the distance I could hear the sound of drums. Of course it was only the drums of the high school parade I heard, but as I gazed at the little bronze cross in the old gentleman's coat lapel it seemed to me that we were in a war; that men and boys were leaving; that battles were raging.

"Were you in a battle, Mr. Whitsett? It must have been a good one, for them to give you that. Tell me—"

"Pshaw, no, I wasn't in no battle. No battle a-tall. I was with Shelby's men, I tell you. I

WHEN SHELBY PASSED THIS WAY

dunno why they give me this thing; twasn't for no battle. I was in lots o' raids though, and I had a battle o' my own once; 'bout Texas, too. Still got th' marks of it. See here."

His eyes brightened and a grin spread across his face as he touched a long scar across his left cheek, extending from his chin almost to his eye. Shelby's Escort was a daring lot of men, and this survivor must have measured up to the standard. Shelby's Men attached to Price's Division had touched this Square, were touching this Square again, with the sound of drums to lend reality.

"How long were you with Shelby and how did you get that scar?"

"Well, you see I didn't go till '64. I wasn't but sixteen when Shelby came through here and I had to go. It was a big day for Bonham when Price's Command come through. We got word they wuz comin' when they left Fort Gibson so we wuz ready for 'em when they got here. They'd been up in Missouri and Arkansas and back through the Indian Nation. Six months or more they'd been makin' raids for food and supplies for th' Confederates an' drivin' th' enemy back wherever they could find 'em. Folks through here had plenty o' meat and flour and meal t' give 'em.

"Th' day they come to Bonham 'bout six or eight of us boys lined up here on th' Square to meet 'em. We'd done made up our minds we wuz goin' with 'em no matter what anybody said. Les' see, there wuz me an' Joe Chiles an'

John Howard and Les Henly an' two or three boys from Sherman an' Cooke County. We tied our ponies to th' hitchin' rack an' come over here to watch th' soldiers. They had their band playin' *Dixie* and *Bonnie Blue Flag* and I dunno how many more of them old songs. We could hear 'em a long time before we could see 'em. Nothin' like a band, honey, to sweep you off your feet.

"Jus' th' way it wuz that day. By the time th' soldiers did get here we wuz restless and rarin' to go. Shelby's Men all rode horseback; right back o' them wuz Gen'l Price ridin' in a buggy. Plenty o' foot-soldiers too, front an' back of both. Guess they looked pretty hard after a year's marchin' thru Missouri but we didn't notice that; th' girls didn't either, honey; they wuz all roun' this Square with flowers, and candies, an' such. Th' women-folks of all ages wuz here that day. Th' Genr'l called a halt for a parade aroun' th' Square. He got out of his buggy and kissed all the little gals, an' some of th' big ones too.

"When th' parade wuz over, us boys jus' rode right on out o' town with 'em. That wuz a peculiar introduction to war, now, wa'n't it —parade an' music an' kissin' th' girls an' babies? But when I caught a sight of Jo Shelby I knew he wuz th' man I was goin' t' follow. An' I wuz never sorry for a minnit. Course we boys thought we wuz goin' t' git into battle right away and save th' Confederacy an' all that. Well, we wuzn't smart enough to know it but th' Confederacy wuz already lost. It wuz gittin' towards winter o' '64 then an' when we got to Arkansas we went into winter quarters.

"I got me a good new uniform, two six-shooters and a sabre an' I did a right smart skirmishin' roun'."

"How did you get a new uniform if the war was almost lost and times were hard?"

"Well, honey, the Govern'ment issued th' cloth an' I persuaded some nice ladies in Arkansas to make it for me. 'Twa'nt so hard." He chuckled as he shifted his weight and stepped out farther on the sidewalk to look for the parade which was steadily coming nearer.

I had not yet learned about the scar across the cheek. That Mr. Whitsett had an art at feminine persuasion when a lad of seventeen I did not at all doubt. There was so much sparkle to his conversation now that he must have been a dashing lad with his two six-shooters and his sabre, held in readiness to save the Confederacy.

"But how did you get that scar? Was that just a skirmish for food, too?"

"Well, in a way, it wuz an' in a way it wuzn't. It happened one evenin' when we wuz sent out to drag corn. You see we wuz skirmishin' an' foragin' all th' time for ourselves an' for th' men on th' other side o' th' Mississippi. While we wuz out in a farmer's field I heard some men from Louisiana that wuz in our Command talkin' about Texans. They wuz sayin' th' Texans wouldn't fight but that they loved to brag about it. I dropped my corn and yelled out at them to say that agin an' they'd fin' out. One man laughed and said I wuz only a kid. He put his hand on his pistol an' tol' me to shut up. Well, honey, I didn't shut up. I jus' took my sabre in hand.

"With that th' other fellow changed to his sabre too an' we went at it, hot an' heavy. Pretty good fight we had too. Other fellows come up an' stopped us. Both of us wuz out an' our sabres wuz broken but Bud Phillips, that wuz th' man I wuz fightin', wuzn't as mad as when we started. 'You're all right, kid,' he said to me. 'You'll make a soldier.' My face wuz pretty bloody an' I had t' go to th' surgeon's tent to get it dressed. Th' nex' day Phillips an' I had to go to town to get our sabres repaired. Had t' git a pass of course an' we went along together, friendly as you please."

The old gentleman hung his cane upon his arm and began digging in his coat pocket. He pulled out a small piece of paper as he continued. "Always carry this in this coat an' I want to show it to you—it's a copy of th' pass."

I glanced at a photostatic copy of a brisk order which read—"All guards and picquets of the C. S. A. will pass Hayden Whitsett and L. H. Phillips of Shelby's Escort to have sabres repaired and return this evening."

J. Smith, Orderly Sergeant
N. M. Langham, Captain Commanding

"To get sabres repaired." How strange it seemed to be reading that as we stood there in the fall sunshine and listened to the martial music of a band approaching! Conscription had just passed and National Defense talk was flowing from radios and press. I returned the pass with a fervent hope that there would always be men like its owner.

"When I got back to Bonham th' town wuz full of Yankees but I wore my new uniform that wa'n't so new by that time but still good, an' my two six-shooters an' my sabre. Yes sir, I had a great time goin' round th' courthouse that day. Th' soldiers wuz nice t' me an' nobody tried t' stop me.

"It wasn't long after that that I decided I'd better get some schoolin' an' I went t' school still wearin' my uniform an' my six-shooters. I asked Mr. Carlton, th' teacher, if I could come t' school wearin' my guns as I wuz uneasy for fear th' Yankees might come after me an' he said certainly I could come right along. That's th' way it wuz." He smiled again and continued. "I managed to learn somethin' too, even tho' I wuz a great fellow t' hunt deer an' buffalo. Well, honey, that music sounds mighty good, jus' like it always did; an' look at this pretty little gal that's leadin' 'em. She's a dandy, ain't she?"

A high-stepping drum-majorette of the high school came into view just across the street. She was leading her band from North Main and at the Square she accented a little more her part in the parade. The music was a college march but it was a rhythm that soldiers could march to, also. The drum-majorette twirled her baton into the air above her and, high-stepping, scantily-dressed, caught it with a flourish of success and skill. Her short white satin skirt twirled about her knees as gracefully as the baton twirled above her head. The gold braid on her jacket glinted in the sunshine. Her short white boots looked like the stream-lined version of the war boots of the Sixties.

Around the Square and past the reviewing stand they went. Placards and floats shouted their pride with slogans like—THANK YOU SAM, FOR THE DAM—and WE APPRECIATE YOU, SAM. At the northeast corner of the Square the voice of a radio announcer spoke to all the Red River Valley, saying— "This is a great day for Bonham, folks. There's a big crowd here on the Square, and Bonham is proud of its part in this celebration. Here they come—let's have a look at them—"

Around this Square passed many men. I was seeing not only drum majors and majorettes, congressmen, clubmen, farmers and publishers, but Shelby's Escort, and General Price, and foot-soldiers from a year's foraging in Missouri, and eager boys with ponies falling into line. The back-surge of the crowd came up and carried me with it. The wearer of the Cross of Honor was already far ahead of me, marching around the Square.

What a place is the old-fashioned American of it! And what an institution is a good old Square with a courthouse nestling in the middle American parade!

4

— Plain and Fancy Riding —

It's no new story to boast of Texas women's horsemanship but pioneer women of the Red River region executed feats of skill and courage that their descendants of today do not surpass.

Of all girls who grew to womanhood between the Fifties and Seventies none was a more typical example of her life and times than Elizabeth Thomas Darwin. Daughter of the pioneer Andrew Thomas, Lizzie was born in southeastern Grayson County on the farm that was to remain her home throughout a long life.

Wild horses were very common in the days before the Civil War and if a settler needed more stock for farming, trading, merchandise or even for the pleasure and entertainment of his family he just went out and rounded up a herd of wild horses. It was in those halcyon days when money was not required for ownership. There were only the Indians to dispute the possession of them.

Breaking in a horse and training him to his gaits was a masculine sport that appealed to the pioneers. Lizzie Thomas' father had a great many horses at his home near Bois d' Arc Creek. The best of the lot was a little bay pony which he broke, trained, and presented to his daughter when she was twelve years old. He wanted her to ride, hunt and be independent of her brothers when she wished to go to school or to Kentucky Town or the Skillet.

Lizzie was a true pioneer girl, strong, rollicking, self-reliant and gay. She began riding horses with her father or brothers when she was five, but the little bay pony with a white star in its forehead was the very first thing she had ever owned. The pride of her ownership was shown by the care she gave the animal. She fed him choice tid-bits of food; she gave him rub-downs, exercise and long hours of conversation until Brownie became more gentle than the family dog. His answering whinny to Lizzie's call was the signal for a romp of at least an hour between the two. Lizzie decided that if *she* went to school, so must Brownie. She must teach him tricks that would make her the envy of every young girl and boy in the valley.

She began her instructions in the barn-lot where there were fences, stiles and gates. That gave Lizzie the thought that it would be a good idea to make a jumper out of Brownie. She had never heard of anyone of her neighbors having a trick horse like that. She started by dragging backlogs from the woodpile in the yard and setting them up as obstacles. Brownie was willing to practice as long as she brought him rewards of candied honey and bits of molasses candy. In the training process she gradually added log upon log until her father chided her and asked her if she intended moving his woodpile just for the exercise; if so, he could take her and Brownie too, to the fields with him for some real exercise. But she replied that Brownie was not meant to be a plough horse and that she herself intended to be a horse-trainer, not a farmer. Her father said no more and accepted her ambition cheerfully for he was deeply interested in Lizzie's love of horses.

He and all the family were on hand the gala day in September when Brownie walked up the stile and down, daintily posing on each step, and later taking the entire thing in one hurdle.

Lizzie carried a long, supple, hackberry switch which she used to tap Brownie on the ankles for his mincing steps over the stile, and to flourish and twirl in the manner of a circus ringmaster as she imagined him. She wore boots just like her brothers' and one of her brother's suits of homespun shirt and breeches. She informed her family that at her next program Brownie would take the fences as easily as he had the stile.

She set to work in earnest to make her word good, another pioneer characteristic. Sometimes she used a man's saddle and sometimes a woman's side-saddle and sometimes no saddle at all. She loved best to jump upon the old horse block in the lot, call Brownie to the block and leap upon his back without a pause or loss of a step on Brownie's part. She preferred to ride bareback and although she had never seen a

PLAIN AND FANCY RIDING

circus she had read about the bareback riders and her highest aspirations were to emulate them.

When her family next assembled to witness Brownie's tricks it appeared that she had attained her aim, for Brownie jumped the fences, the gates or the stile as his mistress who carried candy in her pockets and a switch in her hand directed. The family applauded vigorously. Who wouldn't have done likewise in witnessing the spectacle—Liz, the spirit of youth, taming, directing, challenging the strength and grace of the animal world?

The only drawback to her accomplishment was that her father insisted that she spend as much time with her books as with Brownie and her mother agreed with him to the letter. Another thing was that they also insisted that she must wear girl-clothes everywhere she went except when riding. Thus Lizzie could only boast at school about her horse and his tricks but it is said that many times on Saturdays and holidays and vacation times her schoolmates came to the farm in Walnut Grove and watched the trick-horse that turned their hearts green with envy.

However, there came a time when what had been fun and play became protection and safety. By the time Brownie's tricks were so routine that he jumped fences, gate or stile with equal willingness and grace, it was spring and Lizzie was fourteen. On a certain Saturday in corn-planting time Lizzie was in the kitchen wondering how she would spend the day. Her mother had just left to spend the day at a quilting contest at Lick Skillet but Lizzie hated the thoughts of spending a Saturday indoors with a ladies' quilting party and she had begged off when a neighbor's wagon stopped at the house for her mother.

"You had best spend the day with your father and brothers in the field, then, Lizzie. You can help them plant the corn. Do not stay long in the house alone and when you do, be sure you keep the doors barred. There's always a danger that Indians might be scouting round in these parts in good weather like this."

Lizzie remembered her mother's cautions and meant to heed them. She had heard the menfolks talking about some Kiowas and Comanches that had been stealing horses lately in the neighborhood of Sherman and her schoolmates said they had come much closer than that; in fact they trimmed the story with their imaginings until the children were looking for Indians in the very doors of the schoolhouse. But not Lizzie; she made the bold statement that she was not afraid; she had seen Indians before and just let any of them try to steal Brownie and she would show them; she'd ride right away from them, that's what she would do. Now on this Saturday morning when her mother had left her with such strict orders to watch out for any strangers, either Indian or white, Lizzie went first to dress up in her brother's clothes for she intended to spend at least an hour put-

PLAIN AND FANCY RIDING

ting Brownie through his tricks and then perhaps she would help plant corn.

As she stood beside the kitchen window giving a final jerk to one of her boots she was horrified to see six Indians within ten feet of the window. They must have come, not from the front way nor from the field way, but from the thicket back of the barn. They were on horseback but were so silent she had not heard a sound. They were slipping from the backs of their ponies and would be at the door before she could reach it to drop the bar. She stamped her foot into the unruly boot and pushed her hair further into the cap and hoped they would think she was a boy. Perhaps they would take food and nothing else. There was still some cornbread in a platter on the table and a bowl of boiled meat. She had a feeling in her heart that Brownie was what they wanted and Brownie was galloping around in the lot now, whinnying in excitement.

Before she had moved a foot the outside door of the kitchen was opened noiselessly and an Indian's face looked at her appraisingly. She stood her ground and tried to stare at him with the manner of a woodsman or a hunter. She took a step and pointed at the food upon the table, but the Indian took a step also and shook his head; so did two others who appeared behind him.

"Horse—take ponies—you too, huh?"

They stealthily encircled her and she made a dash for the door thinking she might escape to the field. But the other three were waiting for her just outside and by grunts and gestures the six drove her towards the barn lot where Brownie and the three saddle-horses of her father and brothers were; the two oxen and two mules were in the field. Now she hoped that Brownie would remember all his tricks! She might outwit the Indians yet if Brownie could do his part—without either bridle or saddle. As soon as they reached the top of the stile she took two steps at a time and jumped upon the tree block as quickly as an Indian himself could have done and whistled for Brownie. The little bay pony came cantering to the block expecting to do his usual tricks. Perhaps he thought it was only another audience to please.

"Go, Brownie," whispered Lizzie as she leaped upon Brownie's back and leaned forward on his neck to talk quickly and quietly in his ears. "The fence—Brownie, and jump as you never jumped before." Her arms were around his neck and her fingers clutched his mane to guide him.

Brownie seemed to sense the urgency of the situation. Intuitively he felt his mistress' needs and he responded gratefully with speed and accuracy. He cleared the picket fence of the lot before his would-be captors realized the white boy's trick. Then they turned and ran for their ponies and jumped upon them to pursue the fleet-footed Brownie. A pony like that they must have. They too could use that trick.

But Brownie and Lizzie had the start. They

PLAIN AND FANCY RIDING

cleared the second high picket fence which enclosed their yard. Lizzie knew if they could reach the corn field, or even the sight of it, they would be safe. "Hurry, Brownie, hurry. I'll make you some molasses candy all for yourself, if I get back to that kitchen."

The Indians were now gaining ground and coming closer but so was her father's corn field. When she could see her father in the field she let out a scream that was also a screech and a howl. "They'll hear that, Brownie; they've got to. They won't think it's me, they'll think it's Indians and they'll be right. On, my darling, on."

True enough her father and brothers did hear her scream. They seized their rifles, for of course they had them beside them. They didn't stop to wonder about the strange sight of Lizzie leading a party of Indians directly toward them. They aimed at the Indians and as quickly as they could re-load they fired again and again. Lizzie and Brownie came on with greater speed. After three or four such volleys the Indians turned their ponies and galloped away and not in the direction of the house either. The men came running and when Lizzie got Brownie turned around she yelled at them, "They wanted our horses, Pa," and led them to the home lot. When they reached the gate she pulled Brownie to a stop. "That's good, Brownie. You'll get your candy but you don't need to jump this time. We'll wait for Pa."

Her father came up, panting. "Well, Lizzie, calc'late I'll git you to train all th' horses. Dogged if it ain't a good trick and handy as a musket sometimes. You ain't so good on shootin' as me an' th' boys but Great Jehosaphat, gal, ye can ride!"

— SOLDIERS IN THE CELLAR —

The mistress of Glen Eden was known throughout the valley for her ability, wit and charm. Her plantation of nearly a thousand acres had a shore line on Red River that afforded ample choice for a good boat landing. That spot had been found in Coffee's Bend, noted since the early Forties for its ferry and its trading post.

By the middle Sixties the mistress of the plantation had buried two husbands and yet remained the competent chatelaine who shipped cotton from the Bend to New Orleans and received in exchange the trimmings and trappings that transformed a sparsely-furnished log house into a mansion on the frontier. Her two husbands had possessed the means but neither the taste nor the efficiency to effect this transformation. Her first husband, Colonel Holland Coffee, was the typical frontiersman who met a violent death when he was stabbed by an Indian in an argument at his trading post; her second husband, Major A. W. Butt, was an army officer who was waylaid and killed by guerrillas said to be members of the famous Quantrell's band. The selling of cotton in war times was often the motive for robbery and murder.

But Miss Sofia surmounted each hardship with a new manifestation of her ability and wit. In the case of her second husband's murder she did not rest until she had the perpetrators under arrest and even though they later escaped she had the satisfaction of knowing that she had done something in the way of justice. Quantrell's men and the James boys were often self-invited guests at her mansion and seldom did they abuse the standard she set up there for their conduct. She continued to send her cotton and food supplies down Red River to Shreveport for the Confederate government to give to Southern soldiers.

Although born and reared in Indiana, Sofia Suttonfield was a fervent believer in the Confederate cause. She had come to Texas as a bride of sixteen and soon had felt the influence of strong supporters of the South. Between the Thirties and the Sixties she became acquainted with a great many United States soldiers who were stationed at Fort Gibson and Fort Washita in the Indian Nation. They came often to Glen Eden to enjoy the hospitality and the friendship of its mistress.

Many are the legends about Miss Sofia's activities in war days but the most popular story is the one about the way she trapped some Yankee soldiers in the cellar of her plantation home. There seems to be no written record of actual fact as to when this incident occurred or as to what Union soldiers were doing on the south side of Red River, but there are a number of people today in the neighborhood of Preston Bend who like to tell the story of how Miss Sofia caught the soldiers. They still take a pride in the glamour of her deeds and they quickly will direct you to her home where you may see the actual cellar of the story. If you are at all skeptical that there was such a person as Miss Sofia you may go to the little country cemetery on a near-by hill where you will find a monument to her memory.

One midsummer's day between 1861 and 1865, says the legend, Miss Sofia looked out the window of her second-story bedroom at Glen Eden and saw a cloud of dust rising from the sandy roadway. She stood very still at her window and listened. She could hear voices and soon she saw the galloping horses of some twenty or more riders. In another moment or two she could see their blue uniforms. She stepped back behind her damask curtains, confident that they would not pass without stopping. It was so still that she could hear what they were saying, and her suspicions were confirmed that they were looking for someone and they were coming in to search her place and to ask her questions.

She caught the words of a raucous voice. "Hey, Cap'n, where *is* that Glen Eden?"

"On a sand bar in Red River maybe, or just ahead on the left, Sergeant," came the answer.

She saw the officer check his horse, take his

field glasses from his saddle bag and turn them full upon the house as if he knew exactly what he was looking for. Although screened by the curtains of her window she stepped farther back into the room so as not to be caught in the circle of his vision.

"Cynthy," she said to the slave who was both maid and bodyguard. "Cynthy, I think we're going to have some more company. But unfriendly company this time; that is, it may be. These soldiers are wearing blue uniforms and I have an idea they've heard of something they think might be here. Better get on down to the kitchen, Cynthy, and see that there's plenty of food in sight and occupy yourself at preparing more. Have some coffee boiling on the stove. You might stir up another cake even though we have cake. Get busy and keep that way, unless I call you, no matter what you see or hear. I always think it is a good idea to feed soldiers, don't you Cynthy?"

"Yes'm, I sho does, but if any o' dese heah sol'jers starts botherin' you, jus' you call fuh me an' I cin git mighty busy in th' front o' de house mighty quick." The big mulatto moved noiselessly out to her duties.

Miss Sofia went over to her bureau and spoke to her reflection. "I'll just put this cameo pin in my collar and throw my blue kerchief around my neck before I go down to receive the gentlemen. Uh-m, there they come. Sounds like they might be in a hurry." Closing her bedroom door she descended the stairway cautiously and slowly, trying to catch more of the soldiers' words before opening the door.

"Any port in a storm, Sergeant, an' if this ain't a storm I never seen one—sand, briers, stickers and stingers."

"I been hearin' 'bout this Glen Eden ever since I been on th' frontier an' I'm pinin' fer a sight o' its pretty mistress."

Miss Sofia smiled and knew that she had been right in adding the pin and scarf to her calico dress of pale yellow with black ribbon trimmings.

"We'll be lucky if we fin' 'er here an' not in Jefferson or Shreveport," said still another voice.

"A moment, Sergeant, while I try the knocker." That must be the officer, for it was an educated voice. She knew that the time for opening the door had come, for heavy feet were pounding on the veranda; they almost stifled the reply.

"Not too long with your manners, Cap'n; we're hungry." The Captain pulled the knocker while their feet and hands banged on the wall and their voices yelled "Open up! Open up! Where is my pretty lady?"

"Augustus," Miss Sofia called softly to the little black boy standing in the hall, watching her. "Open the door."

Augustus slid into position and quietly opened the big, paneled door, taking himself at the same time to a position of safety behind it. When Miss Sofia stepped forward, the chattering voices stopped while the soldiers stared at her in surprise. They had expected resistance. The officer spoke first.

"Captain Dudley and party from Fort Washita, Madam. You will pardon us I hope but we're searching for a detachment of Confederates. You will not mind if we ask you a few questions?"

"Certainly not, Captain, but this is a cotton plantation, not a soldiers' rendezvous."

"I'm afraid we must be the judges of that, madam. We are ordered to take no chances on this trip. This *is* Glen Eden, I am sure, and you are its mistress, Miss Sofia?" She bowed her head as he continued, "Your plantation here on the river's edge occupies a very advantageous position. It is accessible to Indians and soldiers alike. No doubt this is annoying to you sometimes, but we have orders to apprehend some furloughed Confederates and new conscripts who are trying to reach Shreveport with supplies. We know that they have been in the neighborhood of Preston and it's not likely they would pass your place without stopping; now is it?"

Miss Sofia glanced past him at the men already pushing into the hall. There were only the black people and herself at the plantation. If these fellows should make trouble how was she to stop them? Besides, everything depended on delay; she knew precisely the whereabouts of the men they were seeking for she had helped them to escape across the river. This was a

SOLDIERS IN THE CELLAR

moment that would require diplomacy for there was a determined glint in the Captain's eye. He spoke again.

"Come, come, madam, I've been told you are very friendly to Confederates but you've also been kind and hospitable to Union men." There was a sudden stiffening of Miss Sofia's smile which Captain Dudley detected and sought to rectify. "Perhaps, I should say United States army men before the present hostilities began. Your father was a U. S. army man I've heard and your fame as a hostess is well known at both Gibson and Washita. You can save yourself a lot of trouble and embarrassment if you'll tell us now when you saw them last or which way they went."

With greatest composure the Lady Sofia stepped forward. "Captain, you and your men must be very tired as well as hungry. You are welcome to what rest and refreshment Glen Eden can give you." She turned to call to a little black boy. "Augustus, go tell Cynthy to send me the keys; they're in my bedroom. And hurry, Augustus."

A little black shadow appeared from nowhere, seemingly, ducked between the soldiers and disappeared. Captain Dudley decided that the lady was going to be agreeable while playing for time. That was all right too for he thought she was a very charming lady to look at; especially did he like her keen brown eyes that held the suggestion of a twinkle. He would keep her engaged in conversation and thus allow Sergeant Thomas time to search the house for food as well as for Confederates.

"Sergeant, proceed with your search. I'll follow you."

But he didn't, for the lady smiled at him as if she meant to speak. Then she was interrupted by the little black shadow again who spoke. "H'yah de keys, Miss Sofie."

"Thank you, Augustus. Now, Captain, I should be pleased if you and your men also would try some Glen Eden wine. We have some Madeira, too, and a little champagne that we brought from New Orleans last year. Just come this way, gentlemen; I'll show you the cellar first."

She stepped out upon the front veranda, jingling her keys as she walked. The Captain discovered that he must follow her instead of the men. He raised his voice to speak to the Sergeant now standing at the west doors of the great hall.

"Sergeant, the search can wait a moment. The lady wishes to treat you to Madeira from New Orleans."

Pell-mell they came through the front door accompanying the lady across the wide veranda and a portion of the yard to the gallery of the ell. Joyously they watched the mistress of Glen Eden—a lady famous for her charm from Fort Gibson to Fort Washita—lift a section of the porch floor.

"Well, I'll be blowed! Who'd a-thunk it?" Sergeant Thomas was stupefied.

"Reckon you'd a-found this here hidden door, Sergeant?"

The speaker was a rough, burly fellow who leaned against a veranda post and shook with laughter. Before the Sergeant or the Captain could answer with a reprimand the lady of the plantation continued with her invitation.

"This way, gentlemen; just follow me," spoke Miss Sofia, descending the short stairway to the cellar.

No second invitation was needed. There were cries of "yes ma'am" and "thank 'e ma'am" as the men stumbled down the six short steps. The officers tried to exercise a little dignity and therefore came last but the entire company was literally at her feet. On each side of the steps against the wall were two rough benches while in the center of this spacious twenty-foot cellar stood a long broad table. There were shelves too—three rows of them—around three walls. Bottles, casks, jars and jugs filled the shelves, and kegs and barrels graced the corners. Such furnishings made an unreal, gleaming vision to the tired, thirsty cavalry riders of the United States army. They had seen no such cellar as this since they left their Illinois and Indiana homes to join the forces of Uncle Sam. Some of them had never seen a well-stocked cellar like this one. Certainly, it was most unexpected to find it on an Indian frontier or in the wild, rebel country of Northern Texas.

The astonished soldiers heard the lady give

a command. "Go and bring some wine glasses, Augustus. Tell Bill to come here too and serve the gentlemen. Run; be quick about it."

The Captain was the first to recover his composure and assert his control. "Madam—uh—my dear—Miss Sofia—I'd like to say—uh—"

"Don't bother, Captain; permit me to say it for you. Welcome to anything you see here. Bill and Augustus are here to serve you."

Bill, a very old slave with long experience in serving ladies and gentlemen, and little Augustus, his eyes rolling with fear and wonderment, had slid into the cellar unobstrusively and were busily engaged in helping the gentlemen find their chosen liquors. A wild scramble now ensued; there was the noisy clinking of glasses and popping of bottles mixed with the dragging of benches and the rattle of side-arms on the table accompanied by loud laughter and strident voices. Miss Sofia stood in the doorway on the first step and bided her time until the first frenzy had passed. Then she spoke.

"Captain Dudley, may I give the first toast?" She took a glass of wine from Augustus. "Thank you, Captain. Now gentlemen, let us drink—to the *President*."

Quickly was it drunk without question. None stopped to think that the country then boasted two Presidents. If the lady with a twinkle in her eye drank to one president and the soldiers in blue to another, it went unnoticed.

SOLDIERS IN THE CELLAR   55

Ignored too was the disappearance of the lady some time later. No one heard the fall of the trapdoor and the click of the lock. No one but Captain Dudley and he heard those sounds faintly for he was yielding to the spell of a champagne dream. However, he did drop his glass upon the table and run quickly to the cellar stairs. He pushed against the door and called loudly to Miss Sofia, to Augustus, to Bill; but no one answered. Then he realized that the lady had trapped them neatly and securely and that he was too weak-of-will to offer further resistance. He returned to his champagne to complete the oblivion that had already engulfed his men.

As soon as she had sprung the trap, Miss Sofia moved quickly into action. The most necessary thing was to get the word of warning to some Confederates in hiding near Harrison's Bluff on the opposite side of the river. A Captain Graham and ten or twelve men had stopped at Glen Eden only yesterday; she knew their plans of trying to take supplies to Shreveport. Captain Graham was a Texan from the Brazos country and no stranger to Miss Sofia for she had met him in Austin five years ago when he was no soldier. Consequently she had been only too glad to contribute to his supplies from Glen Eden's store of meat and flour. She had no notion of allowing Captain Dudley to acquire those supplies, or the men carrying them. Therefore, she had no time to lose for she knew if the men should break out of the cellar, they would try to find her; failing in that they might try to torture the slaves into telling of her whereabouts. She must take pains that no one, and particularly little Augustus, see her leave the plantation for the landing. The very thought of her hospitality to the Yankees in the cellar made her smile; they had been most appreciative too and would likely remain so for two or three hours. She didn't want to lose her control over them and have them break through the door; no, peace and pleasantness must be kept and the Confederacy must be served.

After looking cautiously about she strolled in a leisurely manner through the back yard to the smokehouse but there her manner changed. Quickly she dropped her keys in the bottom of the big log meat trough and placed some sand and leaves over them. Looping her long skirts over her wrist she stepped out softly and took the path through the cotton field to the river. It did not occur to her that she was attempting a difficult task; she had swum the river many times for her own pleasure and in the urgency of this situation she dared not trust her warning to anyone else. The river was low and that would make it easier by shortening the distance. She came to the bluff just above her own landing and stood looking down at the narrow, winding stream. "Well, it's nothing but a devilish creek to swim but I'm glad Graham's hide-out is just across," she said as she began undressing in the shelter of a post oak tree. There was plenty of quicksand in that winding creek as she knew but not at this particular point—Glen Eden's Landing; the quicksand was a mile or so downstream.

She hung all her cumbersome top clothes in the fork of the oak tree. Her femininity was piqued for a moment to think that she would have to meet Captain Graham looking like a run-away child in its underwear. She threw down her stays, her shoes and stocking and let them lay where they fell. Then she stepped out from her shelter attired only in her pantalettes and chemise. On second thought she turned and picked up a stocking and tied it around her head to keep the wet hair out of her face. She didn't want anything to slacken her speed in swimming the river twice before those blue scouts in the cellar became angry and vindictive.

A quick look up and down the river assured her that no one was in sight as she picked her way down the bluff, trying to protect her bare feet as much as possible. In only a few minutes she waded out into the soft, red sands, then into the muddy red water of the river. With the swift, steady strokes of an experienced swimmer she slid away from the landing.

When she pulled herself up on the shore of the Indian Territory she looked more like a wet and wizened urchin than the mistress of the prosperous Glen Eden. A thicket of underbrush and scrub oak was protectingly close but to herself she was thinking that she knew now something of the way a run-away slave must feel, or soldiers fleeing from an enemy, or prisoners-of-war attempting to escape. That reminded her poignantly of the prisoners locked in her own cellar. How she hoped they were still drinking and sleeping! It was her duty to forestall their waking.

Harrison's Bluff was just above her. She pushed on through the thicket to the shade and shelter of a huge old oak tree. She climbed to the first fork of the tree and then whistled the plaintive call of the mourning dove three times. There was stillness all around her as she waited for what seemed an interminable time. Unless the men had already got away, they must hear her signal. Her eyes were fastened upon the cliff as her ears strained to hear an answer.

Then cautiously, softly, invisibly, the answer came—the same plaintive call three times. She jumped down and stepped out into the open and whistled again, more loudly this time; then she curved her hands to her lips and called "Captain Graham." Almost immediately she saw a man's figure come rolling down the bluff in a shower of sand and rocks.

The tumbling figure landed so close to her that the sand spurted up into her eyes as she spoke: "Captain Graham, you've got to get away at once. A Captain Dudley and twenty of his Yankees from Fort Washita are looking for you on the south side of the river. I've got 'em locked in my cellar right now but I don't know how long I can keep them there. They're on a scouting trip and they know all about

SOLDIERS IN THE CELLAR

you and the men with you, and the supplies you've got for Shreveport. There's no time to lose, Captain."

The man wearing a tattered gray uniform but good Texas boots and hat was astounded at the sight before him. His eyesight was blurred by the sand in his eyes, and dust was filtering into his nose and throat. Anxiety was in his expression as he rubbed his eyes, batted at the dust, coughed and replied:

"I—I expected to see Miss Sofia, or one of her hands. She's the only one knows the signal. But whose child are you? Why, damn it all! It *is* Sofia, or is it?"

"Of course it's Sofia, Captain Graham. Don't waste time now making pretty speeches, or the other kind either. I had to leave my clothes on the other side. I just didn't dare send the message by anyone else. Captain Dudley knows all about you, I tell you, and he's trying to stop you from reaching Shreveport. He and his men came to Glen Eden searching for you. I invited them in to sample the wines in our cellar. Then I locked them all in until I could get word to you. They won't notice it for some time, so I've got to get back in a hurry. I'd like to invite them out peaceably as I invited them in. Both of us have got to hurry—do you understand?"

The captain in gray seized her hands. "I reckon I do, General, and your orders shall be carried out. By George, Sofia, no one but you could have done this so neatly. By all means, you must be very polite to the gentlemen. An' while you're about it be sure an' engage the Captain in conversation an' hold 'im with some o' your tantalizin' remarks. You can depend on it we'll be well on our way down the river inside of an hour. We'll stay on th' north side until we get past Warren. We'll try to reach Honey Grove tonight. You're a true soldier, Sofia, an' we'll never forget this . . . Confound it, you've got th' grit of a soldier but I'll swear I never thought you were so little. I've seen you lots o' times but I reckon I could say truthfully you look *best* this way. I wish time wasn't so pressin'."

She pulled away from him and started toward the river's edge. "Well, it is pressing and there's none of it to waste on insinuating remarks. There are times, though, when I forget being a woman. Today was one of them. Goodbye, Eb Graham, and good luck. I've got to get back to my guests. Don't lose the meat and flour and don't eat it all either."

With the agility of an Indian she darted through the underbrush and into the river, swimming back to the Texas side with undiminished speed and strength. When she began the scramble up the bank she heard a rustling in the woods above her that made her think for a moment that Captain Dudley had escaped and was waiting for her. It was pleasing to find that the noise was only the tramplings of a stray cow, probably from her own plantation. She found her sheltering post oak and hur-

SOLDIERS IN THE CELLAR

riedly got into her clothes again, all but her stays and stockings—those she threw further into the brush for there certainly was no time to wrestle with them.

It was only a few minutes later that she stood again at the cellar door of Glen Eden serene and smiling, jingling her keys in her hand and with her wet hair pinned down smoothly and severely; with dry clothes over wet sticky underclothes to say nothing of the wet gritty sand in her dry shoes. It seemed hours to her since she had escorted her soldier guests to the cellar but she knew that in reality it had been little more than two hours. Very quietly she unlocked the door and descended to the second step.

"Oh, Captain Dudley! Would you like to see the rest of Glen Eden, or continue your rest here?"

She could afford to relax now for she saw that none of the men had noticed her absence. Judging from their appearances they were very content to rest longer in her cellar.

Captain Dudley, however, roused himself instantly to answer her pleasant voice thinking that only a few minutes had elapsed since her last remarks. He glanced at the Sergeant draped lazily across the table, soundly sleeping; at the men also asleep. Then duty asserted her strong control and the Captain awoke fully to the situation. Disgraceful conduct! With a slow grin he realized his own guilt. Long hours of riding in the heat had been victimized by Glen

Eden's cheer. But how long had they been there, he wondered. His watch said five o'clock. Great God! They had ridden in here just past noon. How much did this smiling lady standing on the steps above him know? He slipped a hand quickly into the inner pocket of his coat and was relieved to find his papers there intact. What if she had read them? With a pang of shame he then realized that she very easily might have done so. These southern people were noted for stubborn loyalty. Espionage was an art with some of them. He was remembering the twinkle in her eyes when she had proposed a toast to the President.

"My dear lady, I thank you for reminding me of duty as you so short a time ago reminded me of pleasure. Certainly we want to see the rest of Glen Eden. It is most urgent."

"Then, Captain, I will most gladly show you about. There are a number of things that might interest you. Bill and Augustus can help us too."

Before he answered the Captain turned to the sleeping Sergeant. "Sergeant Thomas! Attention!"

Reaction was quick "Who the—what the—oh—Aye, aye, Sir."

"Get the boys above stairs immediately. Search the place thoroughly but take nothing and break nothing. Come, come, the lady is waiting. I'll join you shortly."

He joined Sofia on the back veranda. "And now, my dear Mrs. Coffee or Miss Sofia—I

SOLDIERS IN THE CELLAR 63

hear you called by both names—I wish to see everything, even the smokehouse and the barns."

"Certainly Captain. I am usually known by the name of Coffee since Colonel Coffee made this entire district so well known. We are right proud of our cotton plantation here in the wilderness.

"You should be proud; yes, of many things. Wilderness you may call it but I am sure no one ever passes through it without your knowledge."

"In a way, that's right, Captain. You see my first husband, Colonel Coffee, conducted a trading post near here for many years, well, up until he was killed by an Indian trader. It's always been a sort of meeting place; so it's not surprising that you heard of it."

"Indeed, we've heard a lot about it at Fort Washita and even more about the beautiful young widow who is its mistress. There are stories about her popularity with soldiers and her entertainment of them. I shall be glad to go back and add my bit to those stories and swear to the truth of every one of them. I'm glad I found the place all right but I didn't come trading and I didn't come calling. I came for information and I believe this is the place to get it. Briefly, there are some Confederates making their way through your wilderness to Shreveport carrying supplies for their army. They must have stopped at Glen Eden. We know they are in this region somewhere. There is a chance to trade something, Miss Sofia, after all.

Give me the information about your recent callers and a nice reward is yours. Good money too—gold."

The Sergeant and his party had reached the kitchen and were making a terrific noise of clattering dishes, rattling pans and rough voices. Miss Sofia appeared not to hear any of it and answered the Captain in a tone of amazement.

"Why, Captain Dudley, you amaze me! How could you have heard so many strange things about me? I'm afraid you overestimate my popularity. It's so easy to be mistaken in the information you get these days for we all get so many unreliable reports. For instance, you probably won't believe it but I'm really telling you the truth when I say there are very few men in this country now except Indians, blacks, and the old, old men left behind. All our young men, as well as older, are in the Service in Arkansas and Louisiana. I'm sorry but I never learned to be a trader. Colonel Coffee was, but I only know how to raise cotton. It's too bad you have had all your worry for nothing."

"That's all right, Miss Sofia; you did your best to alleviate our worries and fatigue. Yes, and I daresay it's people like you that keep those men in Arkansas and Louisiana."

"I hardly know what you mean, Captain. I have no husband and no brother in either place. I have friends in many places. Now, shall we continue our search to the smokehouse? I see the Sergeant is taking his men out there and

I want to show you the bullet-holes left by some Indian fighters long ago."

Quick-witted and also stubborn, thought Dudley as he followed her. At least he would not let her out of his sight again. When they reached the smokehouse he watched her very closely and listened to her Indian stories while the Sergeant conducted a detailed search. He was really enjoying the fleeting expressions in the dramatization of her stories and found that he was wishing that he had nothing to do but watch her and listen to her. When they returned to the house and the great hall he was still perplexed about a situation he couldn't control; how were wars fought with beautiful women? Alas, his military tactics did not state.

The Sergeant interrupted his dilemma. "Search completed, sir."

"Find anything, Sergeant?"

"Nothing of value, sir, except a lot of good food in the kitchen which I couldn't keep the men from taking, sir."

"Oh, but they are welcome." Sofia smiled graciously at the Sergeant. "I know it is hard to get good food when you are away from the Fort."

"'Deed it is, Ma'am. You're due our thanks for both food an' drink.'"

Captain Dudley decided to accept his defeat. "All right, Sergeant, we'll ride on immediately and cross the river at the nearest point." The Sergeant saluted and withdrew to the front yard but the Captain lingered. "And now good-bye, my dear Miss Sofia. Thanks for the refreshment, the entertainment and those delightful stories of the past. It's been a pleasure to meet you. I shall not forget it but I hope we shall meet again." He stepped back and saluted her with a half-serious smile on his face. "You have defeated me gloriously this time, Madam. I accept it but there may be another meeting. May I ask you one more question and hope for a truthful answer? Is it feasible to cross the river here at your Landing?"

"There are some who try it, Captain, although I've heard there is an under-current and the Indians say there is danger of quicksand. It might be better farther down. Good luck, Captain Dudley."

They walked across the cool veranda. She watched him mount his horse. Men came running with pieces of cake, baked ham and chicken. They jumped on their horses with glee. Good forage like this beat capturing Johnny Rebs any day. She heard one of them say, "Where next, Sergeant? Any more places like this roun' here?" as they galloped down the drive between the catalpa trees.

Captain Dudley lingered still another minute. He rode close to the veranda. "Big risks bring big rewards, Mrs. Coffee. We cross the river *here*. My orders are imperative." He noticed the extraordinary sheen to her hair in the late afternoon sunshine. It looked as if it might have been wet and pasted closely to her head.

She raised her hand to him. "I respect your

SOLDIERS IN THE CELLAR

sense of duty, Captain Dudley; you must always be the judge of that. But take plenty of time and care in crossing. So sorry you had this trip for nothing."

She watched him until he reached his Company and disappeared in the rising sand. Let them cross the river here—Graham and his boys were well away by this time and in no danger of pursuit. She turned back into the hall and barred the door. She must get Bill to clean the cellar right away and restock it; it offered a good entanglement for marauders. Wet clothes did give one such a nasty, sticky feeling. She smiled and called loudly to Cynthy. "Get plenty of hot water, Cynthy. I'll need it!"

The guardian of Glen Eden resumed her role.

6

— Mystery of Black Hollow —

There was once a man in Cooke County who held both the admiration and the fear of every resident of the county. People say he was a handsome man, a charming brunet with blue eyes who was slender and tall to the height of over six feet; they say too he was a cool-headed fellow, daring and deadly with a pistol. There were two women besides his wife who were in love with him and there were times when it was difficult to know which of the three he loved best. He was a popular man with the men too; they elected him to the office of County Clerk again and again until he seemed to be invincible in politics; none dared oppose him.

It all happened in the days of the cattle drives to Sivell's Bend when the stage lines ran through Black Hollow, when the railroad was still as far away as Sherman and when the Western Hotel was the center of life around the sandy Square.

Two men lingered over a drink at the bar. In the Seventies that bar was as good a bar as you'd find in the valley. Often there would be music furnished by some famished traveling musicians or cattle-drivers, or cowboys in from the range. These two men dawdling over their whiskey seemed gravely concerned over some matter too serious for loud talk. The proprietor of the Western had tried to muscle into their conversation a time or two and had discovered that they were only arguing about the robbery at Black Hollow. That was such common talk that he could overhear it at any store or street corner or at the courthouse. Consequently, he ignored the two and devoted his attention to more likely customers or to those who at least might know something new. Everybody knew about Black Hollow. Some talked it; some didn't.

The bar at the Western was in the main or front room of the hotel, as was the custom in so many hotels where the clerk behind the desk was also the dispenser behind the bar. The hotel was a large one, probably as large as fifty rooms. It stood at the northwest corner of the Square of the fast-growing cattle center, Gainesville. It was a two-story structure with long verandas above and below, each trimmed with the gingerbread banisters which were the unfailing sign of prosperity and art.

It was the meeting-place not only for travelers but for the citizens as well. The County officers usually stopped in at the Western when they left the courthouse to hear the news brought in by stage, to play a game of cards or dice, to drink and to chat about the women and the men who were not there. There were women and young girls in Gainesville who remembered distinctly occasions in the last ten years when they too had been allowed to congregate in the Western. That had been when they were "forted up" in the hotel because of Indian raids. Although none of the womenfolk desired another Indian raid there were some who sighed for the sociability that they got when they were "forted up." Indians were still close enough to make a repetition of that congenial state a likely possibility. When the Comanches and Kiowas went prowling by the light of the moon seeking horses, the women and children of the town—not many at that—were wakened and hurried to the hotel where they were locked in securely while the men went out to meet the foe if possible and at least to drive them off. Then of course there were always the tales of achievement and bravery that could be told to an admiring audience when the defenders returned.

But it was not Indians that held the two men at the bar in such serious talk that day in June. Indian trouble was something to make a noise about. Obviously this was something happening in their settlement that had them mystified. The men were heavily armed; two six-shooters apiece hung in their belts. One of them wore a full beard and one a heavy, drooping mustache. The weather was hot and of course they wore no coats but for some strange reason they wore vests, unbuttoned. There was a badge that glistened upon the hanging vest of the one with the drooping mustache. The man with the full beard finally spoke more loudly.

"Tell ye what, Zeb," and he set his glass down on the bar with a bang, "you'll have to go out t' Black Hollow some night an' wait fer 'im."

Zeb of the drooping mustache and the glistening badge only shook his head and drained his glass. "Nope, can't git 'im that way."

A third man joined them at the bar. He had just come in the front door and had heard the last two remarks. He was a tall man and towered above the two at the bar. He had an easy smile about him though, that forestalled any sense of fear that might have flared up at the appearance of an unexpected third party. His blue eyes looked directly at Zeb.

"Trying to catch someone, Zeb?"

"Yep, guess I oughta. Stage's robbed ag'in last night at Black Hollow. Makes th' fourth time in six months. Pesky fellow manages to git away ever' time. Kinder like to know who 'tis."

"Be patient, Zeb; some day you may know, but not now. Let's have another drink." He called loudly to the proprietor and ordered drinks for three and thereafter the morose expressions of the first two gave way to contented, garrulous talk that was harmless.

After a bit the tall man with the clear blue eyes persuaded the two contented gentlemen to sit down at a table by the window. He took a pack of a cards from his pocket and engaged the gentlemen at a game of monte. Anyone that watched him flip the cards and deal would have noticed his long graceful hands. They did not look like the hands of a settler or pioneer. They were clean and white and there was no edging of black dirt under his nails.

"How's all your fam'ly, Gene?" asked Zeb as he picked up his cards. "Had any more kinfolks t' come in on yuh, lately?"

The pleasant smile upon the face of the dealer faded somewhat as he answered, "All my relatives are well, Zeb, and if more of them wish to follow me into this country they will be welcome."

"Well, o' course. We'll be glad t' see 'em. Makes it hard on a feller though t' have so many dependin' on 'im. Good idea you got this county office to help yuh out, ain't it?"

No answer was given to this hypothetical question and the game proceeded for an hour when the handsome man with the clear blue eyes and the graceful hands pocketed the winnings from his semi-conscious friends, looked at his heavy gold watch, and departed. Some travelers in the office looked at him warily and one slunk further back into his chair.

The proprietor remarked after the tall man's departure that the man's kinfolks "were a burden to him; nice people all of them, but they just come in and expected Gene to support 'em." There were uncles and sisters, brothers, cousins and in-laws, said the hotel-keeper, and none of them had ever done any work of any kind, in the opinion of the Gainesville residents. "Why, one of his sisters come up here an' asked my wife how much lard she used when she boiled a ham; Gene come here first with his wife and boy—smart little feller 'bout four—but purty soon the rest begun to follow 'im. They all come from Louisiana as you can tell when you listen to 'em talk. Some say they're part French, but they don't know how to farm and they don't know how to make a livin'. We been 'lectin' Gene County Clerk for the last eight years. Pow'ful pop'lar fellow."

"Does he do anything else besides the County Clerk business?"

"Not as I know of. Why'd you ask?"

The questioner excused himself and asked no more because of the sudden change of voice on the part of the innkeeper. There was a general stir in the office-bar and some went to the door and looked out. They saw a man mounting a big, black horse at the hitching-rack across the Square. The horse whirled round and the man waved a big, black felt hat as he passed the hotel and galloped westward.

"See there," said the innkeeper, "there goes Gene now on his black horse Prince. Well, it's 'bout night-time; better all be gittin' in."

Gene's habits were well known to the residents. Every day at dusk he left the courthouse and the Western, mounted his black horse Prince, and rode westward. He answered all inquiries with the statement that he had a "little family business to see to" and further explanation was seldom sought as Gene had been known to pepper the ground with buckshot where the curious congregated. It was whispered that he had killed a man or two in the old country of Louisiana and that he had been a sharpshooter in the war and had killed no telling how many Yankees! His prowess in Cooke County rested upon the claim that he could drop a deer on sight, could kill several wild turkeys with one shot and knew how to place the deadly one-shot on the buffalo. Men said he did such a neat job of keeping the county's records that there was no use hunting a better clerk; they didn't try.

Gene's horse Prince was often seen tied at the cabin-home of a questionable woman, one who was often found at the Western when men craved feminine company. She had come in with a wagon-train just after the war and when her train went on to California she had stayed to lend her aid in building up the town. It was well known that Gene had a weakness for women. His manners gave him the name of Lothario and his charm gave him entree into any home or society. There was a school-teacher who spent many an evening with Gene's wife hoping to pass a few words with Gene, probably give him a book to read or ask his opinion on matters of business, or make pull candy for them, or just sit and watch him. Gene's wife was cognizant of the situation but if she ever felt concern she repressed it, much as the public would have liked to know.

Some said Gene wrote letters to the teacher and that she had been seen to visit him many times at his office in the courthouse and that sometimes they went horseback riding together. Whenever this story became new, Gene's wife would be seen riding her bay horse, Queen Anne. She made it a point to wait for Gene at the courthouse and the two would ride together in the direction of Black Hollow.

Black Hollow was a place six miles west of town, in a wooded dell of oak trees where the shade was so thick that the road between the trees was always dark. "Black as night in midday" folks said and because of that it was considered a dangerous spot and few people ever went that way alone. Even the stage drivers feared the place. 'Twas not the overland stages that went through the Hollow but a short mail line from Sherman to Denton and beyond. For at least six months there had been a lone highwayman who had given the drivers cause for worry. Sometimes, they said, he only stopped them and disappeared in the darkness as quickly as he had come. Other times they heard bird calls and Indian calls and pistol shots in the vicinity of the Hollow and four times since Christmas they had been robbed of their watches and money and mail sacks. They reported the happenings at the Western where they usually found the Sheriff and other officers and citizens of the town. But nobody knew how to get the highwayman. All the drivers ever told was that the man wore a small black mask and gloves and that he twirled a pistol as easily as a woodsman did a jack-knife. The west-bound stage always went through the Hollow between six and eight o'clock, in the evening. The citizens of Gainesville decided that the outlaw must be some guerrilla who was hiding in the woods, or stealing across the river. Couldn't be Indians for they knew not the trick of mask and gloves.

Some said that it was one of the James boys come back and in hiding, or one of Quantrell's men, who was doing the hold-ups. But it was considered that such a one also would be awkward in gloves and mask. The conclusion reached was that as long as he hadn't killed anyone, or robbed anyone of their county, it was as well to wait for more evidence on the highwayman.

The very recent hold-up now worrying Zeb, the Sheriff with the drooping mustache, was the most brazen and most successful in point of loot of any others to date. There had been a passenger on the stage who had had to give up his watch and money—one hundred dollars in gold with which he had meant to buy cattle in South Texas. He was the questioner who had been so quickly silenced by the hotel keeper. The man had insisted that he had seen the robber clearly in the twilight and that he was tall, and rode a black horse. The driver agreed with his passenger's story. The only fact he added to it was that the outlaw was a half hour ahead of his schedule and that it was not as black as usual in the Hollow.

A month later in mid-July the mysterious outlaw made his next foray on the stage line. This time there were two passengers and again their watches and money were taken, and the mail sacks were carried away on a black horse. Another Black Hollow story was told at the Western.

But the next morning consternation took over the courthouse when the County Clerk did not appear at his office. Word was passed around quickly that Gene was missing. All the merchants of the Square began asking each other questions about Gene's whereabouts. Some wanted to know if a new "batch of kinfolks" had come in the night; others with a sly wink of the eye said maybe Gene had had "woman-trouble." They finally urged the proprietor of the Western to go to Gene's home and make inquiry.

This was done and the full report that Mr. Simpkins, the bustling manager of the Western, brought back was that no new kinfolks had come; that Gene's horse, Black Prince, was gone; so was Queen Anne, and Gene's sister, Miss Clara, said that Gene and his wife had been called to Louisiana on business. All this served to sharpen the curiosity and the imagination of the merchants and of the women when they heard it. The sudden departure of their popular County Clerk was a far more interesting bit of news than the robbery at Black Hollow the night before.

That same evening about supper-time there was quite a crowd in the office of the hotel. The sheriff was there and was again engaged in earnest conversation at the bar. The woman of questionable character who had been known as a friend of Gene's was there. She was behind the bar helping Mr. Simpkins serve the drinks and there was a very sullen expression on her face. It was still early evening but it was most surprising at that when the door opened and the school-teacher who had been so thoughtful of Gene's reading came in.

"Mr. Simpkins, I had to pass through town on my way home and Miss Clara asked me to inquire about a coat of her brother's. He sometimes left it here. If it's here, or any of his belongings, you are to give it to me, please, and I will return it to her."

Before Mr. Simpkins or anyone else could answer there was a loud crash of breaking glass and the questionable woman whose name was Belle raised her voice above the din.

"Oh you will, will yuh? Well, you won't have that pleasure. That coat is at my house. 'Twas there instead of here he kept it. He may have left his books with you but it was his clothes he left with me. Zeb," she walked around and touched the Sheriff on the arm. "Zeb, I'll tell yuh what yuh want t' know about Black Hollow. He's gone now and he won't be back. That outlaw y'all been talking about so long, and the County Clerk you're talkin' 'bout so hard now, is one an' th' same man. Eugene Bundy, that's who it is. I wouldn't hev tol' but when she come in here actin' like she had all th' know I 'lowed I'd better show 'er up.

"If you don't believe me I can show you th' mail sacks after he'd got through with 'em. I helped 'im git away; yep, an' his wife too. There wasn't no leavin' her; never was. He'd always go back to her, so this time he took 'er; figured it was cheaper. That's th' truth, Zeb. You'd as well know it now."

The school-teacher slipped out the door while Belle was delivering her phillipic, and it was more than a week before she was seen on the Square. Zeb found the mail-sacks in a barrel beneath the windows of the County Clerk's office. He found a piece of paper tied to the top-most sack which read "Zeb, I told you that some day you would find out about that Black Hollow highwayman. Now you know, but I served the county honestly. Gene."

Five years afterward the Galveston *News* carried a news item which said that three outlaws had been killed while attempting to rob a train in southern Missouri. The name of the leader was given as Eugene Bundy. But Gene's popularity and charm were remembered at the Western for many a day.

7

— KENTUCKIANS' RENDEZVOUS —

*O' come with me to the vanished town
Which once was called Kentucky Town!
Cotton grows rank in the village Square—
That one-time rattling thoroughfare
Where wagons, ox-carts, post-horse and stage
Contributed each to history's page.*

*Merchant and soldier, bandit and belle—
What stories they know—if they'll only tell!
Stories fair and stories rare
Will echo thru' the Village Square
In tones both harsh and tender—
If Today's not there to hinder!*

* * * * * *

Finus Vittitoe knew the place when he was a boy. He used to stand on the southeast corner of the Square and watch the stage unload. At home he stopped many a time when he was hoeing corn to listen to the sound of the stage horn. Even today he leaves that same field when Memory's stage horn calls. If he listens well perhaps he'll catch that vanished story. Here he comes now—tall, slender, picturesque and colorful in high boots and felt hat. He speaks in quiet tones; let us listen.

"My grandfather was with th' first wagon-train that come here in 1850 from Kentucky.

He built a flat-boat and floated his goods and his family down th' rivers—the Salt River to th' Cumberland, to th' Mississippi, to th' Red River at Shreveport. He was a great friend of Doctor Heaston and helped him plat this town. There wuz just a few families that had got together at Jefferson. They decided to stop here because they liked th 'lay of th' land, and th' rich, black soil. So they laid off th' town and named it Anne Eliza, for th' little daughter of Doctor Heaston. And that's its name today but you'll only find it in deeds and records. You can look at 'em in th' courthouse to prove it. Sorter like folks with high-sounding names —a nickname suits 'em better. They say this town grew up pretty fast. More people came from th' Rollin' Fork and joined up with these here an' more an' more begun filin' claims an' buyin' land while it was cheap. Nearly ever'- body wuz from Kentucky and folks begun to call it Kentucky Town—just a little spot of old Kentucky out here in a new country. My grandfather said nobody bothered to say Kentuckians' Town which they wuz told wuz proper. My father grew up here an' said *ol' K. Y.*, an' that's what I said when I wuz a shaver.

"There wuz lots o' business here in th' days just before th' war an' just after th' war; it wuz a lively place. Out there where you see cotton in the Square we used to have big bonfires on th' 4th of July an' Christmas, an' everybody fur miles around would come. Sorter like a big party.

"There wuz stores all roun' th' Square an' right over there on th' east side we had a little ol' justice court. We called it th' courthouse; it wuz mighty little but it did th' work. We had two big dry goods stores! Batsell and Reeves on th' east an' F. M. Dyer's on th' west. Two saloons wuz here, an' wood shops an' blacksmiths' shops, an' groceries, an' a boardin' house an' tavern where th' stage stopped. It kept th' freighters mighty busy haulin' lumber from Jefferson, over in East Texas. Some of th' lumber they cut right here but most of it wuz freighted from Jefferson; all th' stock an' supplies fur th' stores wuz brought in th' same way. Ever'thing wuz shipped by river boats from Saint Louis, New Orleans an' Memphis to Jefferson; some small boats an' flat boats could come on up Red River to Sowell's Bluff an' Preston. But freightin' to East Texas wuz a mighty good business then. Still is, they tell me, even though it don't come here any more. Looked like they wuz goin' to have a big town here, same as Sherman, Paris or Clarksville.

"But along come th' war. Business jus' folded up. Th' men an' boys all had to go to th' army an' th' women an' children all had to make clothes an' he'p feed th' army. They tell that th' women roun' here did fully as much as th' men in their war service. I wuz jus' a baby then, one o' them war babies you always hear about. I wuz only ten months old when my father went to join Walker's Division in Louisiana but my mother tol' me how she had t' plough, and hoe an' chop, besides her weavin', spinnin' an' sewin'. All her neighbors did th' same. Folks roun' here sent a heap o' flour t' th' army. One reason fur that wuz they had such a fine mill jus' over there a mile or two south of Kentucky Town; yes sir, Weber's Mill wuz known all through th' valley, an' as fur south as Dallas, an' beyond. No wonder, fur it wuz one of th' finest mills in th' state an' one of th' first t' have a steam engine.

"Th' women-folks made good crops an' made lots of wheat. Th' mill bein' so handy made a big demand fur wheat. Sometimes they got as much as $12 a bushel fur it an' government buyers would come in here an' buy up th' surplus crop. They'd often get up a big, free shipment t' send t' Walker's Division. Uncle Jake Weber wouldn't charge nothin' fur millin' th' wheat an' they'd get some teamster t' haul it fur nothin' to Jefferson or Shreveport.

"Uncle Jake an' his brother Uncle John, come here from Cincinnati an' they wuz two of th' finest machinists you ever saw. They had come over from Germany an' had run a mill over there an' had made a little money. They come out here an' set up th' first steam engine aroun' here, or in th' county I 'spect. They built a big, three-story buildin' like a northern barn right out there by th' side of th' creek but they didn't use no mill wheel fur they brought their equipment with 'em. Dozens of people used t' come there an' camp out until they got their wheat groun'. They shipped flour all over Texas. My father wuz workin' fur 'em when he quit t' join th' army. He used t' haul flour t' San Antonio; tol' me 'bout takin' four thousand pounds at one time t' San Antonio where it wuz re-loaded onto a mule-train fur Mexico.

"Them Webers kep' th' mill runnin' day an' night an' every'thing wuz always as spick an' span as a woman's parlor. They wuz so neat an' clean that ever'body marveled at it. I used t' spend a lot of my time at th' Mill when I wuz a little tad. You can't find a piece of it now though, an' I guess I'm th' only one that could show you th' spot where it used to be.

"Th' war come an' went but th' Mill kep' runnin' right along. When th' men come back home they found it wuz th' biggest business there wuz roun' here. Then th' dry goods stores, blacksmiths' shops, an' saloons took on fresh life an' it looked like there wuz goin' t' be a good town here sure that time. But no! No such good luck come our way. We got th' Military sent in here t' give th' folks th' Iron Clad oath an' th' Freedmen's Bureau. My father an' th' other soldier boys had been braggin' about keepin' th' Yankees out o' Texas. When they heard about th' surrender of th' armies east of th' Mississippi they didn't ever think there'd be any Federal soldiers here. But here they come, thousands of 'em, all over Texas. We had a comp'ny camped down here at th' Skillet, 'bout four miles from K. Y.

Wasn't no chance t' go ahead with business then. Nobody had any money, th' men couldn' vote, an' couldn't raise nothin' but trouble.

"Then lots o' cattle commenced passin' through here; people wuz drivin' 'em north through Preston an' th' Nation; of course cattle thieves become common; while some men wuz busy catchin' up wild horses, others wuz sellin' buffalo hides. Business on th' Square dragged along but it had a hard time. One day a man wuz killed at th' blacksmith shop on th' southwest corner there because th' owner dared t' ask a man t' pay his bill. Th' fellow jus' turned an' walked out an' got on his horse an' rode away an' nobody ever heard of 'im again; had a family here he left t' fend fur themselves. Another time there wuz seven men hung jus' outside th' village by Bois d'Arc Creek. We heard they wuz cattle thieves an' th' officers in Bonham wuz on th' lookout fur 'em but they didn't find 'em till they found 'em hangin' from th' trees.

"That reminds me of Bill Penn—th' desperado who wuz said t' have been buried kattycornered with th' world, out here in th' ol' cemetery; nearly ever'body in th' valley has heard th' story of Penn. My father has tol' it t' me many times. He thought a lot of Bill; so did ever'body in this community. There wuzn't any more pop'lar people in th' village than Bill's mother, an' sister Miss Letha. He had a good step-father too, Uncle Judge Lindsey I called him. Uncle Judge used t' preside at th' justice court here. He never had no trouble with Bill but when th' war was over an' th' boys come back it wuz different. My father said Bill made a good soldier but afterwards when they sent th' Military in here, he, well, he jus 'couldn't take it, I guess. For one thing, he wouldn't take no sass from a freed niggah. When a niggah got uppity with 'im he knocked 'im down. That put th' Military on his trail. They arrested 'im an' he skipped his bond, not on purpose you understand, but 'cause he couldn't get t' Sherman through th' mud. So his bondsmen had t' meet th' bond an' that wuz hard on 'em; some of 'em had t' put up their supply of corn fur it. One thing jus' led t' another. Bill got sour about th' whole thing an' he took t' playin' a guerrilla game with th' officers. Some said he'd steal an' rob only from those that had it, such as Union sympathizers an' th' soldiers. Th' Military offered a reward fur 'im but it didn't worry Bill. One time his mother asked 'im t' go t' Batsell an' Reeves' store fur a spool of thread. He wuz awful fond of his mother an' he jumped on his horse an' went gallopin' over. He walked right bang into some Federal officers at th' door who tol' 'im they had a warrant fur his arrest. Bill jus' grinned an' said, 'T'hell with your warrant an' such stuff; I come fur a spool o' thread.' He took one of his six-shooters an' peppered th' soldiers' feet; fur a minute or two that is, until th' soldiers could get on their horses an' go tearin' toward th' Skillet fur re-inforcements. Then Bill took th' thread back to his mother before he disappeared.

"Well, things got worse an' worse for Bill; they got so many things on 'im that th' Military begun closin' in on 'im. Some o' th' local people begun tellin' things on 'im too. In a year or so he was mixed up in every fracas that happened in a hundred miles o' here. He finally met his death near Trenton not far from here, over in Fannin County.

"Twasn't th' Military that killed 'im, no sir! Twas th' Sheriff an' a deputy, both of 'em right from Kentucky Town. Bill had known 'em for years an' thought they wuz friends of his. Som'body tol' th' Sheriff that Bill would be at a certain house on a certain night an' th' Sheriff an' one deputy went out to get 'im. When they got there they hid in th' brush jus' outside th' house an' yelled at Bill t' come out. Bill opened th' door, holdin' a lighted lamp in his hands. He didn't see nobody so he set th' lamp down on a table jus' inside th' door an' stepped out on th' porch; he took out one of his pistols an' shot into th' darkness one time when they got 'im. Of course that path of light from th' lamp made his body a perfect target an' they riddled 'im with buckshot from two double-barrelled guns.

"Then they put his body in a wagon an' hauled it back t' Kentucky Town. They drove up t' his mother's house an' took it in t' her. Ol' Uncle Judge come after my father an' told 'im he wanted 'im t' help 'im dig a grave an' bury Bill. I remember well how father tol' us about it—he said Bill's body wuz all bloody, jus' like they had dipped 'im in blood; how his mother an' Miss Letha took on about it an' said Bill had always been good t' them an' that people didn't know how to take 'im.

"Nex' mornin' father went with Uncle Judge t' dig th' grave. That's how come me t' know about that katty-cornered grave story; there wasn't nothin' t' it, jus' like there wasn't nothin' t' th' story that th' officers tied Bill's body t' a wagon bed an' dragged it all th' way home.

"Father said it wuz a cloudy, misty mornin' when they went t' th' graveyard an' th' grass wuz high as his head; so instead of gittin' th' grave on a line with th' other graves that face east they got it a little crossways but they didn't mean t', at all. People that tell you he wuz buried that way 'cause he wuz an' outlaw, jus' don't know. Of course they didn't have no funeral fur Bill; his mother an' sister jus' cleaned 'im up an' put on his old army uniform an' buried 'im. An' that wuz th' end of th' pore boy that would ha' been a good citizen if it hadn't been fur th' war, and th' hard times that followed th' war.

"Yes sir, th' war hit that family pretty hard. There was Miss Letha, Bill's sister an' th' most pop'lar young lady in Kentucky Town, she fell in love with a wanderin' soldier that soon deserted her. This fellow had been in th' Union Army an' wuz makin' his way back t' Missouri. He stopped here fur quite a spell. They said he wuz a mighty handsome feller n' likeable. Miss Letha had a little gold money, an' that wuz what Bill had brought her at various times, an' a nice saddle horse. When they had been married about a month, Miss Letha's new husband took her gold an' her saddle horse an' rode away, an' he never come back. He tol' her he wuz jus ridin' over t' Sherman t' buy her some new furniture. Nobody ever saw 'im or heard of 'im agin. But as long as I knew Miss Letha, an that wuz until she died, she tol' me she always dreamed about 'im an' that she still expected 'im t' come back. She wuz always watchin' fur 'im t' ride up t' th' door.

"There wuz another lady here that had th' same thing happen t' her. That wuz Miss Mary that lived in that ol' house you can see still standin', jus' south o' th' Square. She had some money, as much as a thousand dollars folks said. She married a cousin o' hers an' pretty soon he got on his horse an' rode away for good, after he'd spent all her money, of course.

"Our county wuz pestered with th' Military fur about five years. When they wuz all gone it looked like business wuz comin' back fur good this time. Folks wuz beginnin' t' make some money with cattle an' cotton. Th' Square wuz filled up with both of 'em an' th' merchants wuz doin' th' buyin'.

"But in a year or two they commenced t' talk about th' railroads. One railroad wuz buildin' north t' Sherman an' one wuz buildin' south through th' Nation. Finally th' H. and

T. C. got t' Sherman an' th' Katy got t' Denison—th' new town they had made jus' fur it. That wuz in th' winter time an' by th' next summer there wuz a scramble t' get t' th' railroads. An' that wuz what finished Kentucky Town. Th' Katy decided t' pass us by an' build a town three miles east of us; they named it Whitewright after one o' th' Katy men in New York.

"Some of th' merchants on th' Square begun to move t' th' new town. Batsell an' Reeves moved their buildin' an' all t' th' new townsite. So did a number of others; Uncle Jake Weber died, th' Mill closed down; his heirs sold th' machinery, an' th' roller mills set up at Sherman. Dr. Ray an' Dr. McComb put their office on rollers, an' there went our doctors. The blacksmiths' shops followed suit, then th' boardin' houses an' th' drug stores. Gradually, one by one, they all disappeared an' in th' Nineties th' Square become a cotton field, like you see it today. Funny thing though, th' Square is still public land an' belongs t' nobody an' nobody pays taxes on it.

"Now we got a fillin'-station, an' a store ag'in, facin' th' ol' Square; we got buses comin' through here on good roads. Who knows but what I may live t' see another town on th' same spot? My father an' my grandfather always said it wuz th' richest spot of land in Northeast Texas an' I still believe 'em. This black waxy's been makin' good crops fur ninety years straight. Ain't no wear-out t' it. Be kinder nice if th' ol' town wuz that way, too. Mebbe tis, too; don't you forget that, boy."

With this the speaker who himself looked like a vanishing pioneer turned and retraced his steps toward his own home under the cedar trees on a whiterock hill—the hill that had been cleared by his father and his grandfather in 1850. Truly, there is no wear-out to this rich valley with its black prairies. Even ghost towns can come back; there are many of them in Northeast Texas.

8

— LEGEND OF CADDO LAKE —

Hernando De Soto and his Spanish friends came across this fertile spot in 1542 or thereabouts; La Salle and his French explorers found it in 1687 and tarried long enough to make friends with the people and leave a kindly impression of the white man that proved to be a measuring stick through nearly two centuries; their fondness for the Frenchman's language became a Caddo weakness. Finally the American pioneers discovered this mystic lake of beauty and gradually pushed the Caddos farther back, back into Texas, into the Indian Territory, into Oklahoma, into oblivion.

But the Caddos' Lake remains at the borderline of Northeast Texas and Louisiana, forming a huge water-way between Shreveport, Jefferson and Marshall; connecting the Red River with its little tributary, Cypress Bayou. It's a huge body of water with no logical reason for its being. Fat fish have frisked in its waters for many centuries and still entice the angler to its shores today. It was around this great sustaining lake, teeming with food and encircled by wild fruit and game, that the Caddo Indians built their lodges and tilled their fields.

LEGEND OF CADDO LAKE

The Caddos were never nomads. Why should they be? Life offered them contentment, peace and happiness without pulling the stakes of their teepees for even one day's traveling. Their canoes drifted upon the peaceful waters of the lake and their moccasins trod softly through the thickets of grape, mulberry and dewberry. The swaying touch of the cypress and the fragrant odor of the pines enveloped them as they stooped to pick their chincapins, walnuts and hickory nuts. The mist of the marshes drifted to the cleared spots where they raised corn, beans and yellow pumpkins. They were a friendly people and hospitable; so much so that their wild brothers of the Plains often visited them in the season of green corn.

Their homes were not overnight camping-spots but fixed abodes; their wigwams were usually made of buffalo hides covered over with thatch. The precision of their plan gave the effect of a neat little village of thatch-covered cottages. In the season of cold and rain there was always plenty of well-cured venison, antelope and buffalo meat stored in cellars or small dugouts behind their wigwams. If the supply ran low there was always the fish of the Rio Roxo and their lake. Small wonder that the roving Indians of other tribes found the Caddo villages vacation spots without parallel.

The Caddos were the dominating tribe of an Indian Confederacy that was formed centuries before the ten or twelve States of the white man banded together with the same name and for the same purpose—all isolationists seeking to pursue their ideals of existence. There is a coincidental resemblance to the Lost Tribes of Israel in the fact that the tribes of the Caddo Confederacy also were lost. Another coincidence is that one of the chiefs of the Caddos was named George Washington; he sought to lead his people in ways of amity and peace with the onrushing settlers, pioneers and land-grabbers.

There were ten tribes in the Indian Confederacy; some of the minor constituents were the Wacos, the Tejas or Tayovas, the Keechi, the Anadarko, the Adai, Eyeish, Wichita and Tawakony. Their territory ranged from the Wichita to the Brazos, but the controlling tribe of the Caddo remained between the Sabine and the Red.

Into this peaceful paradise came the white man. Cabeza de Vaca, said to be the first white man ever to tread the soil of Texas, found it as early as 1535, three hundred years before the state bearing the name of one of the member tribes was created. His visit disturbed not the quiet routine of the melon-growers and the corn-shellers. But it was different when the French and Spanish came. Each found the Caddos in the seclusion of their cypress swamp and each left a permanent effect upon their Indian life. The French left language and customs while the Spanish left their coveted horses.

La Salle and his map-maker, Joutel, lingered among the Caddos in 1685; in fact, some members of the expedition were so charmed with the

LEGEND OF CADDO LAKE

life of the Caddos that they refused to go farther with the Chevalier searching for the big river and new lands. They stayed to instill more deeply the French language, customs and manners into the lives of the American Indians along the *Riviere Rouge.*

When De Soto and Moscoso passed this way, the Caddos traded for some of their horses. These Indians were neither explorers nor warriors and made no claims to either, but they were farmers and traders and in this case they probably saw a chance to be the first in the market with a new product. At any rate for several centuries the Caddos raised horses and traded them to other tribesmen who sought their villages along the Lower Red.

Then came the white man, he who was called "the homespun centaur with arms of steel." The Louisiana Purchase opened up vast new territories of the United States which these "centaurs" felt in duty bound to take and civilize. As early as 1815 white settlers began filtering into the new empire of the Upper Red. One of the first white men to come was Nick Trammel. He found a strange, big lake after he left the little settlement of Baton Rouge, at the mouth of Red River. To cross this lake there was an unusual, natural raft of trees and driftwood. There was no ferryman to charge him toll and there was no sound of hammer or axe to indicate construction. Neither was there any boatman to take him across or to tell him about the lake. He only saw the canoes of the Indians drifting upon the waters of the lake. He waited; he made friends with the Indians and followed them to their village and visited with them many moons. From them he heard the story of the Big Raft and the lake it protected.

"Many moons ago, white brother, there was a great shaking of the earth with the sinking of the ground and the rising of the water. The Great Spirit frowned upon His people, and the Indian hid himself in the moss and covered himself with the trees and the leaves of the forest, but the earth belched forth smoke and water; then it sucked in trees and rocks and said no more. Many of my brethren were drawn into that great Mouth and were never seen again. Ever since then, white friend, we have the big lake and the big logs around it. Indians' moccasins make a path across the logs which we call the Caddos' Trace."

In a little while this crossing became known as Trammel's Trace for Nick was a wide-awake fellow who foresaw that there would be many settlers crossing here and that the path would become a great highway. The moss hung deep and heavy and the logs and driftwood made traffic difficult, but Nick saw a chance for business when the moss and the driftwood were cut away. The dismal swamp would then look less foreboding but still dangerous enough to need a guide. He established a ferry and charged a toll.

The name of Trammel's Trace stayed with the big raft, but Nick the ferryman disappeared

LEGEND OF CADDO LAKE 97

and Mark Epperson took his place. Epperson's Ferry operated in the 1830's. Just as Nick Trammel had predicted to himself, the big raft became almost the only entrance to the land beyond the raft—the upper Red River country. Mark Epperson made a lot of money from the anxious pioneers and settlers who probably thought they were stale-mated when they reached the big swamp and welcomed a chance to pay toll to get out. The State of Texas recognized the invaluable assistance of Trammel and Epperson in bringing settlers into the State by erecting a monument-marker in 1936. And the name of the Caddos was added to the expression of public gratitude.

Along in the 1840's rivermen discovered that steamboats could navigate the big lake and Cypress Bayou as far as Jefferson. Another good business opened up. Nothing hindered progress this time—Epperson's Ferry was over-powered by the sheer force of men and machinery, and the Caddos had long since ceded all their lands to the Government and retreated to a spot on the Brazos where they established their villages. Now the smoke of the "Lizzie Hopkins" and the "Iron Queen" mingled with the mist of the swamp and the chug of the paddle-wheels silenced the ripple of canoe oars. New Orleans was brought closer; some of its luxuries adorned the walls of pioneer homes. Texas shipped beef, buffalo hides and cotton in exchange. The steamboat era on the lake made Jefferson a city of thirty thousand. That era ended with the War Between the States.

In the aftermath of poverty the people waited for another man with a bright idea for a business venture that would restore their former prosperity. None came and steamboats attempted to ply their trade when they could find any, but money was gone, luxury was gone, initiative was gone.

Then before ten years passed, the new Idea appeared. It was Railroads and it labeled the lake, the raft and the steamboats as the useless accoutrements of an age that was dead and gone. To prove the strength of this opinion its promoters had a bill put through Congress ordering the destruction of the big raft because it was an impediment to the progress of agriculture. The raft was dynamited and the lake was closed to water traffic. Thus did the Iron Horse take revenge upon the river-boat. Again the moss closed in and the lake was unmolested except by trappers and fishers.

But in the 1930's there was a marked disturbance of the lake again. There was a great belching forth of smoke, and water, and rocks just as the Indians had said there was when the lake first appeared. There was also a mighty rising of the water but there was no sinking of the earth. This cataclysm was man-made and so well manipulated that the lake belched forth gold—gold and more gold—in the form of slick, black oil.

Seekers of the magic money surrounded the

lake, demanded that it give forth oil to them, dared it to stop, sank more and more oil derricks until it was studded with them, as solidly as a birthday cake. The lake accepted every challenge, responded to every test.

Today little motor boats chug steadily as operators and owners of the liquid gold glide from derrick to derrick to inspect their holdings. The oil pumps purr contentedly while the oil flows on. This was more than half a century after the Caddos had been dislodged by the State of Texas from their home on the Brazos and had become lost among the vanishing tribes in Oklahoma. But those first Caddos in their home along Red River were right when they said their big lake was a lake of mystery.

9

— Paris Fantasy —

Herein lies a true story which has such a flavor of the fantastic that the effect is a pleasant, eerie mixture of the real and the unreal. It magnifies the incredible integrity of the men who made this valley and all Northeast Texas; of men in troubled days, both white and black, who manifested inspiring patriotism and devotion. It is almost a saga of Northeast Texas for it was likely duplicated innumerable times by unsung men of the valley who believed in justice and liberty.

* * * * * *

In 1862 there was a student in MacKenzie College at Clarksville, Red River County, by the name of Jimmy Breckeen. The college, a Methodist institution under the guidance of the Reverend MacKenzie, was the chief learning center of Northeast Texas. There were many boarding students who came by wagon and horseback to spend a year or more in Clarksville where the classics and the arts were expounded by ladies and gentlemen of taste and skill. When Jimmy arrived there from Lamar County in the fall of 1861 (as ambitious a student as could be found on the MacKenzie roll), he was quartered with three orphan boys, ranging in age from fifteen to twenty, who were the wards of the Reverend MacKenzie and for that reason enjoyed special distinction. Jimmy and the MacArley boys enjoyed each other's company as they studied their Latin and arithmetic at the big, round center table in the big square bedroom with its two big four-poster beds.

And then came war and secession to disturb their peaceful pursuance of learning and the arts. Texas seceded despite the pleas of its Governor and joined the Southern Confederacy. Soldiers in uniforms began passing through Clarksville and usually they picked up a few recruits from MacKenzie College.

Jimmy Breckeen was disturbed. No longer could he sit at the round table and study *Ray's Arithmetic* or *Caesar's Wars* in peace. One night he told his roommates he was going to enlist.

"Back home they're raising a Company of Cavalry and I'm going to volunteer. They say there's going to be a Conscript Law in Texas and I won't wait for that."

Bill MacArley, the oldest of the three, protested. "Don't be so hot-headed, Jimmy. This isn't Virginia or Georgia. This is Texas and that war is not coming here. Just hold on."

"Are you boys going to stay here and wait for the Conscript to get you?"

"We're not worrying yet. If the law is passed there'll be lots of ways to claim exemption. Better stay with us, Jimmy."

"I'm going to Paris tomorrow and sign up. This war isn't coming to Texas because we ain't going to let it. We'll meet 'em at the border and tell 'em so."

Jimmy left MacKenzie and became a member of a Company of Cavalry that was riding eastward into Arkansas. Like nearly every Texas soldier he had his own horse and he knew how to ride. He was only seventeen but there were many of the same age in the ranks.

Before he left Paris with Captain Perkins' Company his father gave him a new horse that cost him dearly. Seven hundred dollars of Confederate money and a mule were given for the little sorrel pony that was to be his faithful carrier in the war years ahead.

That first winter when his Division was quartered north of Fort Smith, Arkansas, in tents that had dirt floors or in cabins that had been slave quarters he thought many times about his comfortable room at MacKenzie College. He had letters from the MacArley boys telling him that the school was operating as usual. Typhoid fever broke out among the soldiers and Jimmy fell a victim of it. As yet he had done only scout duty and engaged in a skirmish or two with the enemy but there'd been no big battles to win. This war had not the glory that he had dreamed.

When sickness overtook him he thought it only temporary. But the days went into weeks and Jimmy lay listless with fever. Some of his comrades crawled down to the river bank and brought back thick green moss from the Arkansas and placed it under his blanket for a bed. Surgeons and stewards gave him a little quinine and turpentine to break the fever. They sometimes gave him boiled water that had the flavor of squirrel, for the boys went squirrel-hunting and came back to camp to cook boiled squirrel for their sick comrades.

Captain Perkins noticed Jimmy's condition. "Jimmy, boy, you must get up from there if you're going to be riding with me" he would say when he visited the tent and looked down at the wasted form of a healthy boy. As soon as he reached his own tent he wrote a letter to Jimmy's mother back in Lamar County and sent it by the first man leaving on furlough for East Texas. In it he urged that she send for Jimmy if she wanted to see him alive.

Jimmy had lain on his moss bed so long that he was almost paralyzed; still he felt a spark of life run through him when he looked up one day to see the smiling face of George, a Negro from his home plantation. George was his faithful friend, his nurse, his playmate, his body-servant who had wanted to come with him when he enlisted but Jimmy had begged him to stay at home and help the folks with the farm work.

"I dun' come fuh yu', Mist' Jimmy. Your ma, she say fuh me to bring yuh home an' we's ah-leavin' heah tonight. I'se gwine take yuh out a' heah; take yuh home an' gib yuh some'p'n t' eat. Yes suh!"

Jimmy didn't remember much about that ride back home except that the weather was cold and that the Arkansas River and the rough, rutty roads were partially frozen. George had a hack and two good mules, and Mrs. Breckeen had sent along so many blankets, quilts and pillows that Jimmy thought it was the smoothest ride he had ever taken.

They had to spend two nights on the road before they could reach Red River. They made camp on the roadside those two nights; that is, George made camp. The first night he wrapped Jimmy in all the blankets he had; then took his own blanket to add to the others to make Mist' Jimmy comfortable where he lay on the seat of the hack. George made a huge fire and sat beside it all night to keep himself warm and to see that no one bothered his young friend and master. A six-shooter and a rifle were at his elbow. The second night it was the same—a faithful watch beside the campfire of a half-delirious soldier.

On the third morning Jimmy, in one of his conscious moments, smiled weakly at George, who was trying to feed him hot gruel.

"I'll never forget you for this, George. I've loved you all my life and I always will." His eyes filled with tears and his voice trembled. "If you ever get home with me I'll tell my folks how good you've been."

"Dat's all right, Mist' Jimmy. You gwine

be in Paris fuh yo' breakfast tomorro'. Yes, suh, if dese mules kin get us dere!"

They did get to Paris that day but Jimmy was too delirious to know it. For nine weeks he continued to drift between two worlds. There were times, however, when he realized he was at home and that his mother was giving him good food. That good care finally pulled him through, and young Jimmy walked the streets of the Plaza again.

It was not much walking for he walked on crutches with George's assistance. His old friends hardly knew him. He had weighed one hundred and sixty pounds when he rode away with Captain Perkins' Company. Now he weighed only seventy-two pounds and there was not a hair on his head. But his determined spirit was invincible and to his friends who pleaded with him to get a discharge for disability he laughingly said he'd be going back pretty soon.

Go back he did, when the blossoms of May perfumed the valley and dry sand rose from the hooves of his little sorrel pony. George had taken good care of his pony while Jimmy had been at home and it seemed that both horse and rider were anxious to smell the blood of battle. The little sorrel was tied to the hack when they left Arkansas but Jimmy was unconscious and always in his delirium he was wanting somebody to get his horse before it was stolen. Now he patted the horse's neck in gratitude that they were together again. There was good Confederate money in Jimmy's pockets, too; his mother and father wanted him to eat something besides hot-water cornbread if money could get it.

"Now Jimmy," his mother had said, "you try to get some milk and eggs from the people in the country. Surely somebody must have eggs and milk—if you explain to them that you have been sick."

"Yessuh, Mist' Jimmy, if yuh don't, we'll come and bring yuh an' de pony back agin' effen dey don't treat yuh right. I don' know what dey's tryin' t' do anyhow—'sturbin' us like dis."

Those were mighty pleasant thoughts to take along, Jimmy thought. When he rode through Clarksville he saw MacKenzie College, but he didn't stop. It already seemed a long time since he had studied with the Mac-Arley boys. Someday though, when the war was over, he meant to get some more schooling.

Captain Perkins and his comrades welcomed him back to the Command. There were no soft spots in his company and Jimmy sought none. In a few weeks he was riding through the canebrakes and swamps of Arkansas. There were skirmishes with the Federals and once there was a battle at Cabin Creek. But Jimmy was hardened now; the more severe the sacrifice the more he thrived upon it.

Two more years went by. The Federals still could not get into Texas; Confederates went without tents, without food, without shoes and

PARIS FANTASY

without money but they remained invincible in their zeal, and immovable in their loyalty. Jimmy remembered his typhoid fever and many times rode the little sorrel pony to near-by farm houses to beg or buy something for sick soldiers. Twice he was invited to eat a real meal before he returned to camp.

Twice he was wounded but counted himself lucky that he did not lose a leg or an arm. Anything less than that was not worth worrying about. He didn't ask for a furlough, he didn't ask for a discharge although he was entitled to either. The Federals gave up in disgust about Arkansas and Texas and went back to the safety of their occupied cities. Texas had not been entered.

Jimmy didn't have to send for George but once, and that was when his company was dismounted and he sent his little sorrel pony home. There was not enough corn to feed horses and men too, and Texas had too much cavalry.

Finally, the war ended. The Texas troops were mustered out at Hempstead, and men began their search for homes and relatives. It was a time of confusion and demoralization. Men grabbed ammunition and supplies and made off with them as their just dues. They had kept the Federals out of Texas in time of war, only to hear that now Union Soldiers would be sent in times of peace. Military rule was the 'boogie man' that turned their thoughts toward anarchy or exile.

Jimmy, three comrades, and two officers,

started north together—three hunded miles or more to Red River. They secured a hack and two mules, ammunition and guns. "Cabbage on to 'em, fellows. They're as much ours as anybody's."

The Major and Captain upheld them, in fact, helped them secure the hack. The officers still had their own horses to ride. On the second afternoon of their trek northward the Major remarked, "We'll ride on ahead, boys, and get a good camping place and wait for you." The two officers galloped away.

The boys in the hack looked at each other in astonishment a short time afterward when they heard the unforgettable sound of guns.

"I thought that bang-banging was over, boys, but there it goes. It may be the Major. Push on, push on, you mules." Jimmy was driving and talking first to the mules and then to the two boys in the hack with him.

In less than half an hour they caught up with their officers. It looked like a battle had been fought in the wooded dell of the pine trees. The Captain called out to them.

"The battle's over, boys. Some of Shelby's men tried to waylay us and take our horses. We resisted as you can see. The Major's lying over there wounded. My horse is killed and the Major's is wounded. We'll make your hack into an ambulance and get the Major to safety and a doctor, somewhere."

"But Shelby's men—Major; they're Confederates—"

PARIS FANTASY

"They *were*, Jimmy. Now they don't know what they are. Some of them are turning guerrillas as the quickest solution. They called us to surrender and the Major answered, 'When we are dead, Sir.' There were about four or six of them. We finally drove them off but this sort of thing is bad for us and for the country."

There was a farm home near that gave shelter and aid to the Major; the other four struck camp and lay over for sixteen days until the Major was able to travel. Thus it happened that they all reached Paris together and enjoyed a welcome such as they had dreamed about.

Jimmy found his little sorrel pony waiting for him at home. "George, it makes me feel good to find my horse in such good shape. My father gave a lot of money for him in the days when we had money."

"Shucks, Mist' Jimmy, de ol' Ma'sa tol' me he dun refused $2500 in gol' fuh *me*. Money don' mean so much, Mist' Jimmy."

"That's what everybody's thinkin' now, all right. Are you going to stay with us then, George?"

"Dere ain't no other place fuh me, Mist' Jimmy. I'll be right heah raisin' cotton fuh yuh."

When the fall season came around Jimmy announced that he reckoned he'd go back and get some more schooling. He mounted his little sorrel pony and rode to Clarksville in September, and this time he rode up to MacKenzie College.

Headmaster MacKenzie came out to welcome him.

"Good afternoon, Sir. I'd like to go to school again but I've nothing but my pony to offer you for tuition."

"Come right in, Jimmy. Your old room's waiting for you. A horse like this will take you through the whole term. Go right on to your room, boy."

When Jimmy entered the room all was the same, even to the three MacArley boys. They had been granted exemption because they were listed as assistant teachers to the Reverend MacKenzie, and teachers were exempt from military service. They looked healthy and fat. Bill spoke.

"Well, Jimmy, I told you the war wasn't coming to Texas. We've got ahead of you. We've finished."

Jimmy looked out the window and saw the Reverend MacKenzie leading the sorrel pony to the barn to await perhaps a sale or exchange.

"Yes, Bill," he answered, "during these three years you've gained an education and I have lost one."

The young man from Lamar had found principles, though, that were to be the chief factors of a long life. He never saw his sorrel pony again and he never got another term of school, but integrity and patriotism rode ever beside him as he watched the valley expand. What a leader for a chimerical country that is not chimerical at all!

10

— EXPLOITS OF ANDY THOMAS —

Indian fighter! Quick of eye and strong of limb; swift of foot and keen of ear! A man of the trails and fitted to carve new ones where none existed—that was Andy Thomas!

He came from Tennessee in the 1830's in company with a train of ox wagons carrying those who sought new, free lands to own and untamed, untouched adventures to explore. One of the company was the distinguished Davy Crockett who later won death and fame at the Alamo but at that time he was only a fellow traveler who was impatient to reach the new and unknown country of Texas.

They entered that country by way of Jefferson and Red River and found themselves in the vast wilderness of Northeast Texas. All that section was known as the Red River Province and extended as far west as the cross timbers and the prairie country. The wagons made their way westward following the North Sulphur River until they came to a grove that was thick with bee-trees. There they struck camp.

* * * * * *

In the early spring of 1835 two men sat talking beside Turner Creek. They were cleaning their guns for they had just brought in a deer and enough wild turkey to feed their entire camp for a day or two. One of the men was Davy Crockett and the other was Andy Thomas.

"How'd you like that job o' carvin' I done on that post-oak tree, Andy?" The doughty Davy's face had a broad grin as he picked up his hunting-knife and gazed at it.

"You done a good job, Davy, cuttin' th' name Honey Grove on that tree. Be there long after we're gone, lessen somebody whacks down th' tree. I wuz thinkin' 'bout that last night when I seen it. This has been a good campin' spot an' some of 'em's calculatin' on stayin' here an makin' a town—Honey Grove—yes sir, that'd be all right for th' name of a town. I sorter aim t' push on farther west t' them black prairies I been hearin' 'bout."

Crockett picked up one of his long guns and squinted at it. "Stayin' here might be kinda' nice for some folks but not me, Andy. I'm a goin' on south where th' fightin' is. Tell ye what—I'll swap ye this long rifle fer one o' yore short 'uns. Figger I need a shorter gun fer travelin' anyhow, an' ye mean t' *stay* in this part o' th' country."

It took a deal of dickering and talk but finally the trade was made and shortly after Davy Crockett left in high spirits for the great fight at the Alamo. In only a few weeks more he had given his life for the cause he had been so eager to embrace.

The camp-ground he had christened Honey Grove because he had found there such a multitude of bee-trees became a permanent settlement and is today one of the pleasantest little towns in the valley. Andy Thomas and his family did not stay there though. It was not men he wished to fight unless they interfered with his inmost ambition—land and the possession of it.

Consequently, he loaded his family and their possessions into the ox-wagon and plodded on toward the black prairies he had heard about. When he reached Preston he found quite a little settlement there and a ferry and a trading post or two. At one of these he left his Crockett gun for a thorough cleaning by a man who said he was an expert gunsmith. 'Twas the first time Andy had let the gun out of his sight and that night at his camp he felt lost without it. He liked the carving on the gun stock, especially the little five-pointed star inlaid with silver. Davy had told him that he carved the star when he was making up his mind to come to Texas and help the folks make a new country; at Nashville he had had the silver put in it. Although the gun weighed twenty-seven pounds and was a little over five feet long Andy did not consider those two things any handicaps and in the first few weeks he possessed it he told his wife Sarah that he expected Davy's gun to be the best friend they'd have in the new country.

When he went to the trading post the second

morning of their camp at Preston, he was astounded the moment he put his hand upon the gunstock. The silver inlay of the five-pointed star was gone. Instantly, he raised an argument and demanded a settlement or restoration but to no avail, for of course the expert gunsmith had gone on to parts unknown. Andy was perplexed.

"I brought this 'ere gun in here to be fixed an' I git th' silver stolen. Why, that's one main reason I traded with Davy—I liked them silver trimmin's. He tol' me he carved that star hisself when he knowed he wuz comin' t' Texas. Up in Nashville he had th' silver put in. I've a good min' t' try th' gun now on some o' you fellers. What are we gittin' to? Stealin' th' silver outa' of a man's gun?"

After that unpleasant experience it can be assumed that Andy did his own gun-cleaning and never allowed the long rifle to be out of his sight for long. This constant gun-toting may have had something to do with making Andy such a muscular man for it is said that the circumference of his upper arm when flexed was the same as that of a gallon bucket —"yes sir, big as a water bucket" said one who knew him well.

Of course, there were other activities that added to his muscular development such as wood-chopping and the clearing and cultivation of land. Andy and his family selected their tract of land in the black prairies and quietly went about their business. Indians, even the

EXPLOITS OF ANDY THOMAS

Comanches and the Kiowas, brought no fears to them for Crockett's long rifle never failed. Andy's skill as a marksman became known among the Indians and they seldom molested his home and, in a way, they respected the fearlessness of the man who was building it.

It was no trick for Andy to make his own survey for he had learned surveying in Tennessee. He surveyed two sections for himself in the then unnamed counties of Collin and Grayson. When he heard of the fate of the Alamo and his friend Davy's sacrifice for the new state he treasured the long rifle more than ever. He thought many times about their conversations on the way out from Tennessee—now, Davy had been killed by the Mexicans and he was killing Indians when they bothered him, and in the meantime surveying and farming new land with success. On November 1st, 1839, three years after the new republic had launched its career, he filed his claim for land with the Board of Land Commissioners of Fannin County. Andy decided that things were getting settled fast and he had better file his claims. It had been all of two years since the new county of Fannin had been cut from Red River County; this was seven years before Grayson was taken out of Fannin, and at the same time Collin was extracted from the still extensive Fannin.

Andy felt that nothing or no one could take his land from him and he settled down more assiduously than ever to the raising of crops and the selling of them to the outside world. His wife, Sarah, was as intrepid a pioneer, as fearless and as capable of meeting any situation, as her husband. She couldn't handle a gun with the skill that Andy could but she was good enough to have qualified at anybody's Skeet Club tournament. When Andy went to haul the crops to market she is known to have stayed at home unafraid, entirely capable of protecting herself, her four small children and neighbor women who might seek safety with her.

Her first line of defense was an axe and a gun; her second line was a hatchet and knives and her third was likely her stove wood and hastily and crudely built chairs or any other piece of furniture that could be seized for clubbing. Not very dainty or feminine tools, surely, but then as now women shared equally with men the dangers and the responsibilities of life; on an equal basis too they defeated those dangers, surmounted those responsibilities and enjoyed their victories with the strength of the sturdy oak rather than the grace of the clinging vine.

There was a time when Andy's wife, Sarah, was forted up in her cabin home facing just such a difficult situation. There were only two women, herself and her children in the cabin when a surprise attack was made by Indians. It was in the late afternoon of a day when Andy and all available men had gone out to drive the Indians back toward Whitesboro, and Cooke,

Denton and Wise counties. The doors and the windows were barred but there were cracks in the walls through which the women could peep and then assure their children that the Indians were going away now and besides no Indian could get in the house while they were watching.

It was probably after such safety propaganda as this that Sarah Thomas turned around to see one of the wide boards of her floor rising gently upward. She gave the signal of warning and caution to the others and poised herself with axe in hand above the moving board. In a moment the head of an Indian appeared—only the head, for Sarah Thomas swung her ax and the head dropped back beneath the floor boards with a thud. To make doubly sure the three women took their guns and emptied a volley of shots through the loose board. Then they set themselves to guard both the floor and walls and doors until their men came back and dragged an Indian's body from underneath the cabin and searched the barn lot and nearby fields. After that Sarah resumed her house-wifely duties with little concern for Indian hunts and raids. Why go searching for them and work up excitement when one could amply take care of the situation in one's own home? Such a woman in any age has always known what to do.

"By gum, Sally kin take keer of herself," Andy used to say on many occasions. He said it with pride, with love and with respect. Yes,

Andy and Sally were a pair of fearless fighters who were destined to accomplish much in taming, civilizing and cultivating a new country. There was only one time in later years that Sally did not agree with Andy in one of his business deals and that was when he swapped a section of their land for a pair of oxen. Sally said that was a waste and she refused to sign the papers of transfer but the deal went through anyway on word of mouth. Possession was a little more than nine points of the law then, and technicalities had not been analyzed and classified by astute lawyers. Andy wanted oxen, and land was plentiful; so he worried no more about it.

Over in Fannin County there was another man who felt the same way about land and that was Bailey Inglish. He had filed for so much land that he felt magnanimous about it. He built a little fort and called it Fort Inglish and invited all the settlers in the county to come and stay there for safety in times of Indian raids and wars.

Andy knew Inglish well. He met up with him many times at Warren and en route to Jefferson when hauling supplies. He always stopped overnight at the fort when making the long trip. Sometimes for the trip to Warren he went on horseback and sometimes afoot. On one occasion when he was going to Fort Inglish on foot he found a young man by the road, badly wounded by Indians. Andy realized of course that Indians were near and that he had better get on to the fort as quickly as possible.

EXPLOITS OF ANDY THOMAS

The young man was not dead, and Andy had no intention of leaving him there for the Indians to finish or to carry away as a captive.

"Come along, m' boy, I'll get ye t' th' fort. Up ye go." He swung the boy upon his back as an Indian might swing her papoose, then picked up his Crockett gun and started. Carrying the wounded boy and the twenty-seven pound gun did not exhaust Andy in the least. His eyes and ears were alert for sight and sound of Indians. Once or twice he had to place his patient on the ground while he put the Crockett long gun into action. He saw some horsemen a good distance away that he thought might be Indians and several times he heard noises that made him think Indians were stalking him in the woods. Finally when he was almost to Fort Inglish he came within close range of one of these skulkers of the woods. Instantly Andy put down the young man and hoisted his gun, although he knew that he had no powder left for the gun. He took the chance that bluff might work, and it did for at the sight of Andy and his gun the Indian darted into the denser woods and disappeared while Andy resumed his trip. He reached Fort Inglish in perfect safety and the young man was treated for his injuries and recovered to thank the Indian fighter and bluffer for his life.

Andy knew the traits and habits of the Indian so well that he once killed one who was hidden in a huge hackberry tree. Being a woodsman and a hunter Andy paid close attention to the sounds of Nature. Game was plentiful in those days and he knew the call of every animal that was common to the region. He had found it very useful in his hunting. He knew too that Indians were the perfect mimics and often used this talent to trick the white man. One day Andy was returning to his home from the old village of Kentucky Town. As he passed the Vittitoe place he heard the sound of wild turkeys. That is, he thought at first he heard the turkey call. He settled his long gun against his shoulder and waited a moment before he fired. The sound had seemed to come from the hackberry trees to his left. He sighted at the trees and listened. Again came the call, clear and true. Almost true, thought Andy, but his ears told him the sound was an imitation, and he fired the gun to see an Indian's body fall swiftly to the ground. There was something uncanny about the way Andy could handle that gun. The Indians knew it and very likely the one in the tree that day had thought he was hidden securely enough to tease the white man with a little trickery.

That same uncanniness of Andy's was manifested another time when he killed an Indian at the distance of one mile. He was standing in front of his home when he sighted the Indian riding toward Kentucky Town. He picked up Davy's gun and aimed. That was all that was needed. It is no wonder that the Indians gave him a wide berth and that no settler was

EXPLOITS OF ANDY THOMAS

his enemy. The gun of Davy Crockett was a long-range one.

The trusty weapon reached as far as Austin on two occasions. Andy was anxious to secure the patent to his land and he figured the best way to get it was to go and get it from the Governor himself and the quickest way to Austin to be absolutely sure of getting there was to go afoot. A hitch-hiking trip in 1852 or '53 was not a matter of walking a few miles and riding many but of walking every one of the 275 miles. Andy had to make this trip twice before he secured his patent, duly signed by E. M. Pease as Governor, in 1854. With this paper describing the Andrew Thomas survey tucked neatly in his pocket he returned to Grayson County.

On both these trips he carried the famous long gun of twenty-seven pounds. The muscular Andy would not have known what to do with the belt or pocket pistol of today whereas the man of today would likely think anybody a fool to carry around a rod like that. As usual, Andy's affairs at home went smoothly during the Austin treks for there was Sally with her hatchet, axe and gun. The Thomas plantation prospered amazingly.

Of all the interesting stories about Thomas though, none is more fascinating than the one about buried treasure. There is something about a hidden-gold legend that strikes a responsive chord in the heart of every age. One day in about the middle 1850's a company of Mexican soldiers stopped at Andy's place and asked permission to camp for the night. They of course were granted that privilege and with it all the hospitality that Andy and Sally could give them.

One of the officers who spoke fairly good English told their story—that they were making their way to Mexico City with a shipment of gold. The legend is not clear about why they were taking the dangerous overland route with their shipment instead of the water route, nor why they had been to Washington—if it *were* Washington—for the gold but it is extremely clear about the amount of gold they had with them—$60,000 in twenty-dollar gold pieces. That's a good little amount of money even by today's figuring and to the ears of 1850 it was astounding!

The morning the soldiers departed Andy saw them off and wished them well; yet at the same time he felt some misgivings about their trip. Would they reach Mexico with their gold, he wondered. It was a long seven hundred miles to the Rio Grande.

It was not at all surprising to him therefore when one of the soldiers stumbled into the Thomas yard the very night of their departure calling for help. He could speak very little English and he was badly wounded. Andy and Sally took him in and dressed his wounds. It seemed, as well as they could understand his story, that the company had been surprised by Indians only a short time after they had set out that morning. When they saw they were

EXPLOITS OF ANDY THOMAS

being encircled by the Indians the soldiers hid the gold in a small cannon and buried it on a rise just above Pilot Grove Creek. The Thomas' understood that much very well, also that every member of the company with the exception of the wounded one who told the story, had been killed.

In a few days the Mexican left, saying that he must go on to Mexico and get help to return for the gold. Andy and Sally were so interested that they made it a point to inquire about a sick Mexican soldier from every traveler from the south who passed their way in the next six months. They heard from several that the Mexican soldier had died from his wounds before he reached San Antonio.

At any rate nobody returned for the gold. Andy and Sally always looked for some officials from Mexico but the years slipped by and none came. Andy used to say that he was sure the money was buried right on his own farm and that some day he would take out and find it himself.

But the War Between the States came along and then everybody in the county was burying his own bits of gold, silver, family valuables and keepsakes. After the perils of reconstruction had passed and the Seventies and the Eighties came along, the story of the buried gold had dimmed somewhat but still there were parties who came with "mineral outfits" and asked permission to dig for buried gold. Some said it was near the village of Pilot Grove and over there people were frequently digging around on Dixon's Mound for the treasure.

A new angle of the story developed when someone said the gold had been carried back to Mexico secretly long ago, perhaps in war times, perhaps while the Military was quartered in the vicinity. Andy Thomas' grandsons who live on the same farm today do not believe the legend but there is a granddaughter who has searched through the woods many times looking for trees with special markings on them. She has found Indian arrowheads, spurs and bits of bridles but no gold.

About twenty or thirty years ago Mr. R. W. Ball and his brother were ploughing in their field which adjoins the old Thomas farm when they turned up a number of Mexican swords, pistols and bridles, and of course, a large number of arrowheads. Their land is near the creek the Mexican soldier mentioned but they did not believe the story and never bothered to dig further for the buried cannon.

Andy and Sally said if they had only been able to understand Spanish they might have gotten better directions for finding the treasure and obtaining it for their family and their descendants. But so far as anybody knows the fortune of $60,000 still lies buried somewhere in the Andrew Thomas survey.

Andy himself lived to the good old age of ninety-six and his body lies buried in the Vittitoe Cemetery very near the grove of trees where he shot the Indian that tried to fool him with a turkey call.

Andy had three sons, but it was to his daughter Lizzie that he entrusted Crockett's gun. He cautioned her to take care of it always. Throughout her long life she did so and she passed on to her two sons the same admonitions for the care of the long gun. It has never been exhibited or loaned to any museum.

That land for which Andy filed in 1839 is still owned and cultivated by his grandchildren. A granddaughter lives near the old home which her grandparents built. And that long gun of Indian days rests today very quietly and sedately in a comfortable clothes closet in the attractive modern brick home in Whitewright of Mr. Pearcy Darwin, Andy's grandson.

Andy and Sarah Thomas were straight thinkers—they knew what they wanted. They got it and secured it for those who followed them.

— Pioneer Child —

A little girl was playing in the muddy waters of Pecan Creek, on the edge of Gainesville. So intent was she in riding her stick-horse to the brink of the two-inch stream and then urging her yellow hound into the stream that she did not hear the approach of a horseman who pulled up short and watched her for a moment before speaking.

"Howdy, little girl. What might ye be doin!?"

"Drivin' cattle across th' river, Mister. There's Indians on th' other side and Chock don't want to go. But I'll make 'im if I have to fire my pistol an' scare 'im." She pulled a hand-carved wooden pistol about six or eight inches long from her rope belt and looked up at the horseman menacingly.

The horseman grinned. "Don't blame ye, sister; that's th' only way to do 'em. You seem t'· know things. Ever hear of a place called Sivell's Bend?"

"Oh, yes sir, my pappy is a Doctor and he goes ever' where. There's another Doctor at Sivell's Bend—Doctor Ligon. You know 'im?"

"Well, no, but I calc'late I will. I aim t' spend

a spell with 'im. But ain't ye skeered of Indians, little girl, like Chock, there?"

"No sir, Chock jus' don't know what I'm playin'. Indians ain't mean aroun' here any more. I wish they'd make another raid like they did once. I had a good time when we were forted up in th' hotel. It started in th' night. My pappy was gone an' my mother waked me up an' told me th' Indians was comin' an' we was goin' t' th' hotel. All I remember that night was th' way my mother's fringed shawl tickled my legs as she pulled me along. I was too sleepy to be scared but th' next day we had lots of fun. Our mothers let us eat anything we found in th' hotel an' do anything we wanted to while they were looking for th' men to come back. When they did come back we had more t' eat and ever' body danced." She looked closely at the buttons on the horseman's coat. "Where'd you get those buttons, Mister? Are you a soldier?"

The rider relaxed in his saddle and laughed. He threw one leg carelessly across the saddle horn. "Bless my buttons! You're a likely young'un for a girl. You ought t' been a boy. I believe you'd speak up to anything. What's your name, gal?"

"My name's Douglas and I've got four brothers, and no sisters. My pappy named me for a man called Stephen Douglas. What's your name, Mister?"

"Well, they called me Little Allan because they thought I wuz such a little runt. They don't think so, now. Well, Douglas, my name's

Scotch, so they tell me. I'd better be gittin' on. You might ask too many questions. By George, how old are you anyhow?"

"I'm eight an' me an' Chock and Tony, my pony, ought t' ride on off an' leave you. I asked you two questions an' you didn't answer. My mother says that ain't polite."

The horseman laughed again, very loudly and straightened himself in his saddle. Then he took off a crushed felt hat and bowed very politely. "Well, Douglas, I'll tell you. I'm a sort of a soldier and sort of not but these buttons belonged to a real soldier. I thought they wuz right pretty too. That wuz one reason I took his coat. Shiny, ain't they? Tell ye what— ye like 'em so well, I'm goin' t' give ye one to remember me by." He took a long vicious-looking knife from his pants' pocket and snipped off one of the metal buttons and tossed it down to the little girl who stood astride her faithful wooden steed.

Little Douglas caught the button and forgot all about driving her cattle across the river. She hurried home to show her pretty button to her mother and brothers. She waited until after supper when the Doctor had come in and had pulled off his boots to rest his feet. She saw that her mother was carding cotton and her brothers had just got in from the horse-lot. This would be a good time, she thought, to spring her surprise. She dug it out of the pocket of her homespun dress and put it on the table near her father. "Look! See what I got today."

"Why, that's a Yankee button!" exclaimed her father. "Where'd you get it?"

"From a man that asked me if I knew where Sivell's Bend was. Said he was goin' out there for a spell. I asked him if he was a soldier and he said 'sorter.' He jus' giv' me that button 'cause I kep' askin' 'im questions he said."

Her father laughed before he frowned. "He told the truth, I've no doubt, but where did you meet him? In your yard or on the Square?"

"We was playin' over on Pecan Creek. I was pretendin' that Chock was a herd of cattle and I was drivin' 'im across th' river."

"My dear Douglas," and the firm note in her father's voice made the little girl pay strict attention. "Don't let me hear of you going as far as that creek to play again, no matter how many cattle you think you have to cross. Gainesville is too full of soldiers, Indians, and outlaws to think of straying where your fancy calls. You might be stolen any day. Your brothers should heed this warning also. And you had better play quietly at home like a little lady."

"Yes, pa," she always said *pa* when she was very solemn, and *pappy* when she was glad. "Was this man a robber, you reckon?"

"Very likely. There have been a number of robberies in the neighborhood of Sivell's Bend lately. Some of Doctor Ligon's cattle and horses have been stolen."

Little Douglas retrieved her button from her father's conversation and prized it all the more to know that it had belonged to both a Yankee and a robber. It gave her some good ideas for a game the next time she went with her brothers to play on Pecan Creek. That would have to be some time in the summer, for her pa had been firm about her playing like a lady. She heard him now talking about going to see some sick soldiers. Her pa was always doing that. She heard some folks say the war was over but the Yankee soldiers had just come to Gainesville. She had seen a lot of them on the Square and now when she heard people talking about Yankees she knew what they meant. She could see them most any day. She thought they wore fine clothes, all new and clean-looking. Her pa and her brothers didn't have any such clothes. Clothes, clothes! She wished she had a new red homespun like Teenie had!

"The young fellow was badly wounded in his little skirmish with the robbers. I was out at the camp to see him today. I really don't see how he is going to get well. He just can't have the care he needs." The Doctor sighed and bent over to rub his aching feet.

"Then why don't you bring him here, Nat? The boys and Douglas can help me look after him."

Douglas began to listen when she heard her name called. "Will I have to take care of a Yankee, pa?"

"He's a very sick young man, my dear, and a long way from home. You'll do whatever your mother tells you and be sure you do not pester him with questions, do you hear?"

"Yes, pa, but I do hope he can tell me some good stories about robbers and battles."

Their conversation about the wounded soldier was terminated quickly for there was a loud "Halloo" at the front gate. She knew what that meant. Pa would be going out to see somebody sick. Soon, she saw him pulling on his boots and with a cheerful "Look for me when you see me" he went out into the night. All she could do was to take her Yankee button and go to bed.

The next day she stayed very quietly at home playing with her rag doll after she had helped her mother with spinning and sewing. She begged her mother to make some red dye so that she could have a dress like Teenie's. Her mother didn't seem to hear her, she was so busy cutting bandages for pa to use on sick folks.

Douglas was digging a cave in the sand under a pecan tree in the front yard that afternoon when she saw her pa and four or five other men coming toward their gate carrying what looked like a sick man on a pallet. Seemed like there wasn't any end to sick folks; they always had some at their house to work on.

The newest patient at the Bomar home was the wounded Federal soldier whom the Doctor had described the evening before. It took weeks of patient care to make a convalescent of him. The Doctor went his usual round of ministrations among the soldiers and among the residents, in town and out, along the river's bends and through the prairie's grass. It was a perilous time, just after the close of the War Between the States and the Federal soldiers quartered in Gainesville, the town between two creeks—Elm and Pecan—to enforce the terms of the surrender or to subdue any outcroppings of what they called the rebellious spirit were not popular in Cooke County. It was a common thing for highwaymen of all sorts to hold up some soldiers and rob them of their clothes and money. It was in just such an encounter that the young man recovering at the Bomar home had been wounded. The Doctor was one person who went everywhere unarmed and unharmed. He fought only two foes—Disease and Suffering. The patients whom he treated at his home were left to the supervision of his wife and family. When he brought in this case he told them the boy was Willie Files from Michigan and that it was up to them to see that he went back there alive.

The Doctor's wife was adept at this sort of thing; she could tend a patient and tend a house and children without sustaining a case of nerves for herself. When Willie Files was able to sit up and notice his new environment it was mid-June and the mosquitoes were humming over Douglas' forbidden Pecan Creek. One of her duties now was to amuse and entertain their guest from Michigan. She brought her home-made toys and played round him in the summer shade, giving at the same time full explanations of her imaginings. She staged corn-cob fights for him, she described the stage-coach drivers who passed through Gainesville, and impersonated Indians and cowboys. She did the same for the story of the horseback rider who gave her the button, but with exaggerated accuracy. He had, in her story, become a daring outlaw whom she had faced down and driven off with her questions.

She showed Willie her souvenir button one day whereon he exhibited renewed interest in the story for he declared that it was exactly like the buttons on his own coat, the one he had worn on the night he and three companions had been held up.

"Perhaps that was *my* coat the fellow was wearing. I'll bet it was. Where did he say he was going, Douglas?"

"Sivell's Bend and Doctor Ligon's; maybe, cross th' river. Why? You got another coat, haven't you, Willie?"

"I reckon I have, if I ever get out o' here. Clothes are not bothering me much now. Do *you* bother much about clothes, Douglas?"

"No, cause we don't get many. Little girls don't have new clothes. Sometimes our mammas dye their old ones till they get th' prettiest colors. I been beggin' my mother for a red dress for a long time but o' course she always has to wait on th' sick. I bet I get a red dress when I get grown."

Willie sighed and said "Of course." He gave her back her Yankee button and watched her playing with it—throwing it up, catching it, throwing it up and catching it. Finally he spoke again.

"When I leave here I'm going to give you something that you'll like better than you do that Yankee button."

"Oh, Willie, what is it?" She stopped her playing. "Will you give me one o' your pistols or belts?"

"It's something that will go with that red dress if you ever get it, and it's something I can do while I'm sittin' here twirlin' my thumbs an' itchin' to get out and hunt outlaws and Indians again. Say, I heard a story since I've been here about some little girl that had a red dress and lost it to the Indians. Who was that?"

"You mean Teenie? Yeah, I know 'bout that. Her pa let 'er go with 'im to town one day an' there was some friendly Indians on th' Square. They had come into town from 'cross th' river to trade some things. Tennie wore her red dress and some o' th' Indians asked her if she'd trade her dress for some rope they had. Well, Teenie liked her dress a lot but she thought she could get her mother to make another one for she knew there was still some red cloth at home. She wanted the lariat th' Indian had, 'cause she wanted t' play cowboy and learn calf-ropin'. So she made up a story to go home. Her pa sent her on home with her brother Ted. Teenie had t' tell Ted about her trade so as t' get 'im t' go back with her. He said he would if she'd let 'im use th' lariat too. Teenie changed to her old dress as fast as she could an' went runnin' back to th' Square with Ted hurryin' her all th 'time. Th' Indians was still there an' Teenie found th' one that had wanted th' dress an' offered it to 'im for th' rope. He grinned an' took her dress right quick and run off an' jumped on his pony. Teenie lost her dress an' didn't get her lariat either. Her ma an' pa punished her by makin' her wear her ol' homespun. I bet I wouldn't trade like that, though. Did you know th' Indians like t' run off with Mr. Gooding's boy Roger one day, just that same way?"

Willie had to listen in spite of himself. She was so determined to interest him and she was so bright and sparkling while she told it. "Was Mr. Gooding trying to trade his little boy, Douglas?"

"Oh no; Roger run off from home an' when Mr. Gooding found 'im he was sittin' on th' groun' with some Indians right up near th' Square. They was eatin' out of a pan. Roger was eatin' too', an' he had a corn-pone under his arm just like they did. Mr. Gooding started to jerk Roger up when one o' th' Indians grabbed Roger away from 'im and started to run off with 'im. Well, Mr. Gooding had to do somethin' quick. He just dived into th' Circle and grabbed one o' their papooses that was on th' ground, and began runnin' towards th' Square. The Indian that had Roger turned round in a hurry and said 'No, no, trade white boy for red.' Yes sir, Willie, you got t' be careful when you trade with Indians. Don't you do it, Willie. That's somethin' you Yankees don't know how to do, my pappy says."

"It's something the Doctor does know, I'll admit, and and I'll leave it to him when I can. There's your mother calling you, Douglas. She says for us both to come in. Guess you'll have to help this no-count Yankee into th' house. The Doctor will be coming in soon."

A month later Doctor Bomar told Willie he could rejoin his Company and that he would take him out with him in his buggy the next morning. The Doctor's wife was proud of Willie's recovery for she knew that she had had a part in it. She had grown to like the boy from Michigan and she busied herself with telling him how to take care of himself and that he must come back if he had any relapses. The Doctor's boys wondered if this soldier would ever get home for he looked like a mighty weak specimen to them. They had done what their father had asked them to do to help the fellow but they hoped he wouldn't bring home another one for awhile. It was summer and they didn't want to waste their time with waiting on the sick. Douglas hated to see Willie go. She looked on him as her friend and he had been good to listen to all her stories and to tell her some too about lakes and cities in Michigan.

The Doctor's wife saw that Willie had a good breakfast the morning he left. When it was time to go Douglas insisted on helping him walk out to the buggy, although he said he was strong now.

"All right, soldier, we're ready to go." The Doctor picked up the lines and turned to the little girl whose hands were clutching the front wheel. "And Douglas, just because I am taking away your patient is no excuse for you to think you have to go out and hunt robbers or more soldiers today. Mind, you stay home and help your mother."

Willie Files leaned out from the buggy. He was taking something from his shirt pocket. "Here, Douglas, I told you I was going to give you something to go with your red dress which you're going to get when you are grown. Well, I may not be here then, so I'll give it to you now. Every young lady wants a ring, doesn't she?"

The little girl's hands reached up and grasped Willie's gift in excitement. "Oh, Willie, for me? How did you get it?"

The soldier's eyes twinkled. "Well, Miss, I didn't trade for it. I made it from a button. You like buttons, don't you? I made your ring with my pen knife, for I had another coat with buttons. Now you can remember me with two buttons."

The little girl jumped up on the step of the buggy to throw her arms around Willie's neck in gratitude. "Oh, Willie, it's the very first ring I ever had. I'll never forget you for this; never, never, never!"

She planted a quick kiss upon his cheek and dropped back upon the ground for the buggy was beginning to move. When the dust and sand covered the buggy and Willie could no longer see her, he heard her voice saying, "Good-bye, Willie; I'll never forget you, never, never."

She never did. Seventy-five years later she told the story with animation and interest; with a bit of longing too, for the pleasing world of her childhood.

12

— A Path Through the Sand —

Although Jefferson enjoyed the title of Queen of the Cypress in the period of the river boats when Red River was the main port of entry into the hinterland of the Texas prairies and chief shipping point for all the products of the valley, the Queen of the Valley today is Paris, capital of Lamar County. In the Fifties and Sixties Jefferson was dubbed the Queen of Spades by the rivermen, and the sound of the steamboat's whistle was the signal for general assembling on the wharf of Big Cypress, the bayou that depended upon an engineering trick of Nature for its channel; bustling commission merchants, teamsters and freighters predicted that this would be the biggest port and the biggest city in Texas. But man saw fit to blast the big raft built by Nature and the glory of the Queen of Spades faded. Not so with the Queen City of the Valley today; Paris has risen above all obstacles that threatened its growth to reach its present pinnacle of pride.

The phoenix in its peregrinations through the centuries must have hovered above this city that was struggling to express itself in the sandy uplands of Red River, for twice the city has been almost completely destroyed by fire—in 1877 and in 1916. Each time, like the sacred bird, it has risen from the ashes with renewed strength and beauty. That is why you will see so few buildings there with the flavor of age, so little decay, so insignificant a withering. The age is there, but phoenix-like the city is ever-young.

The tentacles of Paris reach far. From its position in the center of the valley it draws its followers from a hundred-mile radius; it is a long way to her nearest rival. It is more than one hundred miles to a city of equal size; go two hundred miles north and you touch Oklahoma City; go one hundred miles south and you reach Dallas and Fort Worth; one hundred miles east lie Texarkana and Shreveport, state-line cities; one hundred and seventy-five miles west is Wichita Falls and the plains country. There's no denying that its position geographically is a strategic one economically. Perhaps this time the chain-store owners, the truckers, the commission merchants and the gasoline venders are right in making Paris the business center of the valley.

Named for what many have called the most beautiful city in the world—Paris, France—there are other bits of history faintly redolent of the fleur-de-lis. This far-inland city that was once a part of New Spain has other reminders of those who sought to plant the lilies of France in a new world. French explorers in the seventeenth century traversed the region; they charted upon their maps the course of the Riviere

A PATH THROUGH THE SAND

Rouge and in the middle of the eighteenth century there was a French settlement established not far from the present boundaries of Paris. Its factual existence is hard to verify but legend gives it the name of Fort Saint Louis de Carloretto. Perhaps it was some such explorer, traveler, adventurer or colonizer who bestowed the name of France's capital upon the mythical city that was being plotted in 1840.

A quiet little gentleman of ninety-four, Mr. James Breckeen, had something to say about the beginning of that mythical city. It was in the early spring of 1941 that he answered a query about Paris.

"Yes, Pinhook's got to be considerable of a city but I remember when it was nothing but a path through the sand. You see, I was born in this county and what I don't remember about this place my father told me." There was a twinkle in his clear blue eyes that held an enjoyment of the past and he twirled a Masonic emblem upon his gold watch chain while he told his story of a path that became a city.

"My folks crossed Red River on Christmas morning of 1836 and my father was given one hundred and sixty acres of land for a settler. I was born on that farm about eleven miles south of here. I've been coming to Paris for a long time but I can remember mighty well my mother telling about the day my father came home and said, 'Well, we haven't got a Pinhook any more; we're a city now and it's Paris from here on.'

"He said there was a Frenchman here who wanted to name it Paris for Paris, France. Everybody agreed, though some of them said Pinhook for sometime after that. We had a good many stores here then and that was why I loved to come to town. My mother liked it too and even though I was a little shaver she brought me with her. Yes, I recollect holding to her hand when there was nothin' but a path of sand in front of the stores. We had the Plaza, even though it was hard to find it sometimes."

"Is it true that you once saw General Sam Houston in Paris?"

"Yes indeed. He was here campaigning for Governor. That was in 1857; I was a boy of about nine or ten but I remember him plainly. Yes sir, I was standing in front of a dentist's office that day, looking through the window at the dentist and his patient. My father and mother were in town, too, like everybody else, to hear Sam Houston speak. He was running for Governor against Runnels. There was a lot of talk about his coming but I wandered off to look at something more interesting than talk, such as the dentist. I figured he was just about to pull a tooth when there was a sudden clatter and noise and we saw a buggy drive up. It was a top buggy with two bay horses and a Negro driver. I remember seeing a tall, robust, dark-complexioned man step out and hearing the people cry 'General Houston!' I don't remember much else about it but I can see that top buggy and the bay ponies just as plain as if

A PATH THROUGH THE SAND

they stood right there today. I'll never forget that dentist either. He was just ready to pull a tooth but when he heard the commotion he put on his coat and stepped outside, and as the General got out of his buggy the dentist met him and said, 'General Houston, welcome to Paris. I'm Dr. Stertzler and I've cured a thousand cases of cholera in one day!'

"That dentist was a foreigner and must have come from New Orleans where cholera was pretty common. I don't know why I should have remembered that statement and nothing more about the speech of the General, but it must have been either because it was so natural or so queer that it stuck in my mind. More'n likely it was because it was about cholera and the dentist's speaking up to the General about it.

"It was in the 1850's too that I was witness to a murder, but nobody ever knew it except my father and me. It was in the summer time and dry and dusty. There was a traveling show in town and I had come to town to see the show. So had my father and my mother and my brothers and sister. Everybody that could get to Paris was here. I was prowling around the store, listening to the men's talk. There was a lot o' strangers in town with the show and following after the show. It was quite a sight to a boy.

"I was standing by the door about five o'clock in the afternoon watching th' folks around the Plaza when all at once a stranger came rushing for the door and a man I knew was right behind him with a double-barrelled gun in his hand. Somehow everybody but me disappeared. Guess they knew what was coming but I didn't. I just kept my eyes glued on Tom and the stranger. I could see a pistol in the stranger's pocket. He was wearing a long coat, a sort of a duster we called it, but I could see the pistol beneath the duster. The stranger couldn't reach for it, for that fellow Tom was crowding him. I remember there was a barrel of saw-dust just outside the door where they had been unloading queensware. Tom began firing buckshot so fast that the man fell over into the barrel of saw-dust yelling 'don't shoot.' Tom just kept on and fired seventeen buckshots into the man's hip before he turned and went back into the store. I slid out of there in a hurry and found my father and he told me to keep my mouth shut or they'd have me for a witness. I wasn't so sure what that would be, but I didn't want to make Tom mad at me.

"We heard afterward that Tom had played cards with this stranger over in Arkansas and the man had taken all o' Tom's money. Tom told him never to come to Texas; and if he met him in Paris he'd kill him on sight; the stranger was with the traveling show and came right on to Paris. They arrested Tom and put him under guard; didn't have a jail here, but a bunch of his lady friends came to visit him and surrounded him, or smothered the guard, or something, and allowed Tom to escape. He got away and nothing was heard of him for years until a man from here met him in a little town in Central Texas. Sam Smith had gone down there to get some cattle; he recognized Tom but he didn't say anything until Tom spoke to him. Tom asked him about Paris and said he was going to come back and stand his trial some time.

"Sure enough he did come back and they held his trial and cleared him. You see there wasn't a single witness there to testify. I still kept my mouth shut. I had learned that lesson all right at the time it happened. Don't guess Tom or anybody else ever knew that I had seen it all and was really the chief witness.

"Yes sir, I've seen a lot of things happen here in Paris: fire, war, murder, politics and business—business and trade all the time. We've got a real city here, just like they said it would be when they named it. 'Twould have been a pity to have let a city grow up here under the name of Pinhook. But Paris—that suits it, and it still suits me."

The little old gentleman arose from his chair and went to the door with me. From there we could see the Plaza thick with trade. Long lines of motor trucks and buses and private motor cars edged their way through the crowds and spread themselves out along Highway 82, the old National Highway of nearly a century ago.

"See that? It's always that way. People and trade. Makes no difference whether it's wagons, buggies or motor cars! We've made a city here."

Nearly twenty thousand people pledge their allegiance to the Queen of the Valley and shout agreement with the citizen of ninety-four who helped to build it.

13

— Quantrell, Guerrilla Chieftain —

"Quantrell's Men! Quantrell's Men! He's *one* of Quantrell's men!" For more than three quarters of a century that call has echoed through the valley. It has been shouted from the dance floor and the courthouse; it has been whispered at the fireside; it has been spoken with pride, with scorn, in fervor, in doubt, in admiration and in fear. It has made William Charles Quantrell one of the most romantic figures of the Texas border and chieftain of all guerrillas, outlaws and bushwhackers that ever infested the Red River country.

During the war years of the Sixties he directed a well-disciplined company of sixty to one hundred men and from all that can be ascertained from both legend and fact not one of the band was ever known to disobey his orders or to protest his methods of organization. That in itself denotes an unusual personality. The man led a sort of Robin Hood existence; northeast Texas, from Cooke County to Lamar and sometimes as far as Jefferson on the Cypress, was his Sherwood Forest. His depredations were directed not against the inhabitants of the valley but against Union soldiers in particular, and against unknown and unrecognized thieves, cut-throats, deserters and like ilk. Although he and his men were often self-invited guests in the best homes of the valley he always conducted himself with the utmost propriety and a refinement of manner which showed that he had not been trained to be a guerrilla chieftain. He was never lacking in appreciation for the favors he asked, either. You need only to read these excerpts from a letter he wrote to Mrs. J. A. Potts of Grayson County to realize that for yourself.

"Madam: Accept my compliments and I beg to present you with some coffee in consideration of your kindness to my men. We are under many obligations to you and your family. When far off and in danger we will often think of the hospitality received at your hands. Should the enemy ever invade your home we will strike a blow for you all. My respects to all your family. Respectfully, W. C. Quantrell."

There is a quiet dignity about the letter that sounds more like a Senator than a desperado. His other traits of character did not come up to bandit-specifications either. He was not the big, husky type at all for he was rather a small man, somewhat below five feet, eight inches in height; certainly he was not a fat man for he was too much in the saddle for that. No, it seems he was the ash-blond type for he is described as having light "sandy hair and blue eyes that turned to violet at times." H'm, those violet eyes have always been considered dangerous and commanding for both sexes. Besides the violet eyes he had another charm in a well-modulated, soft voice. He was never loud and never raised his voice in command, or in anger inasfar as remembrance goes. Such a man could be nothing less than a leader of men.

Quantrell first appeared in the Red River region in the second year of the war, along about 1862. It was not known until long afterward that the motive for his Robin Hood role lay in the fact that back in Clay County, Missouri, his family had been the victims of Kansas Jay-hawkers and William Charles swore vengeance against all Union soldiers and resolved to show no quarter to any of them. So far as records prove, he never did.

His activities in the valley were such that he is well remembered today. You have only to ask the question, "Did you know Quantrell?" or "Did you ever hear of Quantrell's Men?" to receive astonishing replies.

"Yes, indeed; I went to a party once and danced with one of Quantrell's men. They were handsome fellows, and popular too." This was the opinion of a lady in Cooke.

"Know Quantrell? Sure, I knew him," said a man in Grayson. "Sorter little fellow. He wore long hair. I used to see him ridin' down th' road with his long hair flyin' behind 'im."

Grayson and Fannin counties were favorites with him, probably because Preston, Fort Washita, Colbert's Ferry, Sherman and Bonham were the chief points along and near the river for travelers, and for Missourians, Kansans and Iowans especially. He and his men were in Sherman frequently and liked to ride up and down Travis Street and shoot out windows and street lights if there were any; then they would attend a party or dance. Certainly they could furnish the life of the party. You can rest assured that the rest of the guests took their cues from the dashing banditti. In Bonham they are said to have ridden around and around the courthouse many times, shooting at the weather vane on the top of the building, at birds that might be perched on the roofs of the stores, at any target that would prove their marksmanship. However, as far as we can find out, no one ever questioned or challenged their ability along that line. It does seem though that their misdeeds were more often of the mischievous than the malicious order. Quantrell himself was subjected to arrest one time in Bonham, but this local indignity did not last long. When he went in the courthouse for a conference with the judge, the judge looked at his watch and excused himself to go to dinner, leaving his popular prisoner without any means of either detention or entertainment. Of course when the judge returned from his leisurely meal, the prisoner had gone. The judge knew he had gone for he had watched the whole thing from across the street; had seen Quantrell come out of the courthouse and give a signal, a peculiar whistle, which brought all his men from unknown hiding places; saw the pack of them galloping round and round the courthouse singing and shooting at the same high targets.

But there were countless occasions when they aimed at targets not so high. The list of their crimes included horse-theft, robbery, and even murder, to say nothing of free board and lodging they obtained whenever and wherever they pleased. The men often broke up into groups of fifteen or twenty and made camp for several weeks or months at one spot. Yet there always seemed to be some mysterious means of quick communication for they appeared almost magically and simultaneously whenever needed in any of the five counties of their Sherwood. They took horses, money and supplies whenever they desired them, yet if any wandering marauders, or roving Indians or army deserters tried to take anything of like order the Quantrell men rallied round and prevented it by skirmish, battle or bluff. In a sense they seemed to consider themselves the guardians of the valley folk while the young men and older men were off participating in a war.

There was one time they played a dirty trick upon a hostess who had been kind and generous to them and that was when a small group, supposedly four or six, were staying at Glen Eden, the Coffee Plantation near Preston in Grayson County. They repaid with murder the kindness of the mistress of the plantation.

Major A. W. Butts was a Virginian and a disabled Confederate soldier whom the young and charming Mrs. Sofia Coffee, a rich widow, had met and married in Central Texas. He returned with her to her North Texas home and in 1862 or 1863 was foully murdered by some of Quantrell's men. It was in the fall of the year when cotton-picking was at its peak. Miss Sofia worked the plantation with slave labor and that year the cotton crop was a big one. Major Butts set out one day with a load of cotton to Sherman. He rode horseback to make the sale while the Negroes hauled the cotton in a wagon. Four or six of the Quantrell men had been at Glen Eden for several weeks although it is known that the chieftain was not one of them; neither was Bill Anderson, nor Allen Palmer, nor any other of his officers. When the Major failed to return home with the money, Miss Sofia became worried. Early the next morning she mounted her horse and taking several slaves with her went in search of her husband. She found his body on the roadside not far from home; his horse was tied to a tree nearby.

Miss Sofia suspected her non-paying boarders immediately. She rode to Bonham and notified the Confederate Military authorities there and demanded that they arrest the four men at her house. The officers returned with her, finding the four men taking their ease at the house as she had said. The sudden and unexpected entrance of the soldiers made it possible to place the Quantrell men under arrest. They were searched and one was found wearing the gold watch of Major Butts. The officers started back to Bonham with them but they must have lost them somewhere for they were never heard of or seen again. Some said they were simply told to cross the river and stay away from the Texas side until the whole affair was forgotten.

The story that they were banished from the band is likely true, for Quantrell did not tolerate such acts; he disliked gross ingratitude very much as the letter quoted in the beginning explains. Nevertheless, Miss Sofia never discovered what they did with her cotton money.

One of the most peculiar of Quantrell's experiences occurred in Sherman when he prevented a mob of women from making a raid on the Commissary. Some of the war wives and mothers felt that they were not getting their just dues in rations of food and, led by the forceful and fiery Mrs. Belle Savage, they stormed the food depot. The few men on duty gave way hurriedly but Quantrell happened to be making his way across the Square when he heard the commotion. Again that sense of guardianship rose uppermost in him. Either that or he felt that he was being cheated of something or that a dangerous rival was at hand. At any rate he pushed into the building and in the same soft tones he used with men he remarked, "For shame, ladies! What would your fathers, your brothers and your sweethearts think of you? They are with the Army now, fighting as well as starving. Would you stoop to such as this?"

Shamefacedly and hurriedly the women forgot their ideas of justice and slunk away quickly, wondering if Quantrell were a greater patriot than any of them. These suave gentlemen with soft voices have ever had a way with women. But with all that, legend reveals no violent or permanent love affair of the chieftain with any woman of the valley.

When the war ended and the men came back, Quantrell's name did not have the fear and power it once had held. Local conditions were such that desperadoes and guerrilla warfare became common. Union officers patrolled the valley and feuds and killings were frequent and violent. There were the Lees and the Peacocks making it dangerous for a person to voice an opinion on anything or to get out of his house. Men were called to their doors and shot on sight. Bill Penn joined in with the Lees. Frank and Jesse James appeared in the district and thought it admirably suited to their purposes.

All this was too much competition for Quantrell. He returned to Missouri with the most of his band. Not all however, for Allen Palmer married a young society belle of Sherman and another had married a school-teacher. These and many others remained to become permanent residents of the valley, and there their descendants can be found today.

Better for the chieftain if he too had remained, for not long afterward, in the state of Kentucky, Quantrell met his death at the hands of his Nemesis—United States soldiers. They surrounded the barn where he and his men were in hiding. In an attempt to escape the combined number opened fire. He was struck and severely wounded and a few days later he died in a military hospital in Louisville. His men were faithful to the last; a number of them were killed in attempting to carry their chief to safety.

Thus passed another strange victim of war times. Labeled an outcast and a desperado, his name lives on in song and story and probably will for years to come. Many a soldier was forgotten for greater deeds.

14

— THE LADY ISABELLA —

Clarksville belonged to the Clarks. There was never any doubt about that. But more than to any other of them it belonged to Mrs. Isabella Clark Gordon, known as "Miss Ibbie" to hundreds of people. Clarksville, Miss Ibbie's town, is one hundred and seven years old. And from the time Sam Houston visited the Clark home in the 1830's and carved his name on the window-pane of her dining-room to the 1890's when James Stephen Hogg eulogized a drinking gourd she gave him. Mrs. Clark-Gordon ruled the town, and "don't you forget it." Politically, financially, and socially, she reigned supreme. Her rule may have been a bit despotic at times but it was a benevolent despotism gratefully received by the residents of Red River County. So generous was she with lands, houses and property that one historian described her thus— "Nightly, hundreds of people mention her name in prayer."

Yes, the Lady Isabella was prodigal. She gave away land to deserving settlers, lots to residents of Clarksville, endowed every church but one in the town, gave four entire blocks to one denomination, equipped completely an en-

THE LADY ISABELLA

tire company for the Texas war of independence, and contributed supplies, food and clothing to the Confederate armies. But if she gave away a fortune she also retained one.

She came to the Red River country when she was a young lady in her teens and when a fortune could be had for the taking. She lived until the "Gay Nineties" when her country was again a country of peace and plenty. It was in that last-named era of pomp and ceremony, by the way, that James Stephen Hogg, Governor of Texas, visited Clarksville. The Lady Isabella was a very old lady then but forceful. She presented the speaker with a drinking gourd. The Governor launched forth into a peroration of the good lady's graces and of his esteem for the drinking gourd. When he had finished, he boarded the train with the souvenir clasped closely to his bosom. But before the train had reached the limits of the town he tossed it out the window and ironically, it fell in Mrs. Gordon's yard where it was picked up by one of her servants and taken to her.

It is not likely that Isabella was disturbed by the incident; possibly, she was amused by the irony of it. To have known every Governor from Houston to Hogg was a feat that enabled her to read human nature with keenness and pleasure. There is but one other woman in the development of the valley that matched her in fearlessness, initiative, determination and charm. That one was Sofia Coffee, mistress of Glen Eden in Grayson County. The Lady Sofia managed a plantation of a thousand acres, and the Lady Isabella managed a town of a thousand people. Neither was suited to domesticity nor addicted to sentimentality.

That may be doubted when the record shows that each had three husbands. But upon investigation the statement will stand as truth.

There are many unwritten stories of Isabella Gordon, stories that are delightful, pleasing, touching. Turn the projector upon them and you see a figure who pursues with firmness his charted course. Turn the reel again; it's worth beginning at the beginning.

* * * * * *

The story of Isabella Hopkins begins in 1823 when she came to Texas with her father's family. They came from Kentucky by way of Indiana. Her father, Frank Hopkins, was a wealthy planter and his side-trek into Indiana cost him heavily because he could not transport his slaves across somebody's border. Then he struck out for newer country and fewer laws. He settled in the Red River province of Texas in what today is Bowie County. The first home was very near the shore of the Red River, for there were few white people in the country and canoe-travel was the only transportation line open.

Isabella was eighteen then, with a healthy interest in everything. In the first year after her arrival in Texas she was married to a fellow-Kentuckian, John Hanks, who also was seeking his fortune in the new country. But in three years he was dead, and Isabella was a desirable young widow.

So much for the prologue. The real drama of her life begins with her marriage to James Clark in 1829. It seems that Mr. Clark was a man of means and education. He was a graduate of the University of Tennessee and rather slight and frail of stature, and a member of the Arkansas Legislature at that time. When he married the rich young widow with blue eyes and auburn hair, it looked like a political and social life was unwinding from the old world's reel, just for them.

The division line between Texas and Arkansas was vaguely marked in those days and often people were uncertain as to whether they lived in Miller County, Arkansas, or in Texas. The river was the only boundary they respected. There is a famous story in that regard which took place a little later when Texas had made itself into a saucy, young republic. A well-known lawyer, Judge Richard Ellis, and his son lived in the same house and were neighbors of the Clarks. Judge Ellis was sent to the Texas Congress and his son to the Arkansas Legislature at the same time. Probably in this way the Red River folks figured that they could find at least one program they could support. They made up their minds when the Miller County officers came to collect taxes for Arkansas. They refused payment and drove the tax-collector away with orders not to return. The new republic imposed no taxes at all at that time and this wise policy of thrift and economy aroused a great fervor of devotion to Texas. But not for long! The program was revised and a new tax-program substituted. However, the Clarks still stayed with Texas!

James and Isabella had helped Texas win that independence. He went down to fight with Houston as a commissioned officer, while she out-fitted an entire company of recruits and sent them along with her best wishes. Houston is said to have spent his first night in Texas at the home of the Clarks in 1832 and subsequently stopped there many times. It was on one of his visits that he took his diamond ring and cut the "S. Houston" that was remembered through so many years by the family, friends and visitors.

Mr. Clark was a surveyor as well as a planter and a politician. When Houston's men had won the war and the new country was being opened for settlement, Mr. Clark gave a good deal of time to surveying lands for the congress. He received land in payment and in this way added much to his already large acreage. It was on land of his that a settlement was fast growing into a town. Some say there were people there as early as 1828. It is certain that there were a number of houses there in 1833 and when the war was over and Red River County was organized as one of the original counties the town was big enough to boast about. It was never called anything but Clarksville so far as

THE LADY ISABELLA

records show. How could it have been otherwise when its surveyor, owner, and benefactor helped to build it?

This cultured, frail man dealt a great deal with Indians also. He was entirely unafraid of them whether he met them in his valley to trade or on the trail as guides in his frequent surveying trips. One day in the spring of 1838—nine years after his marriage to Isabella and two years after the independence of Texas had been proclaimed—he looked out across the high, rolling plains of the Llano Estacado and made a sudden decision. He called his guides and servants and began packing his books and instruments. He had had enough of surveying for awhile. He said to Uncle George, his body-servant and slave: "George, get ready; we're going back to Red River. Miss Isabella may need me and I know I need to see her."

The tent was folded, the mules were packed, and the party set out but the trip was an arduous one. The rains set in and James in his anxiety to get home did not stop for weather. A new baby was expected and he fretted about it as much or more than Isabella. She had had four children already and the process never seemed to inconvenience her or to impede her activities very much. But each new arrival merited a momentous welcome, thought James Clark.

"I'm afraid the little tike will get there before we do, so hurry, Uncle George. We've got to push on."

His premonition was right. A new son was in his home when he arrived—James, Junior, Mr. Clark apologized to his young namesake for his delayed welcome and to Isabella for his absence. His life in Clarksville had never seemed as dear to him as it did at this time.

But the festivities of his home-coming and of the arrival of James Junior were shortened peremptorily by illness. Fatigued by his hurried trip from the plains and weakened by exposure, James Clark was stricken with an infection of the throat. Soon he was dead from it, despite the frantic efforts of his family and friends. One of his closest friends was a young physician who attended him, Doctor George Gordon, another Kentuckian and a frequent visitor in the Clark home.

"Isabella," said James one day when he had felt the end was drawing near, "if you should marry again, and I think you will, I'd rather you married George than anyone else in the world."

The Lady Isabella protested vigorously at the idea and at that time the thought of remarriage was almost sacrilegious. But there came a time when the wealthy young widow, then thirty-three, altered her viewpoint, oh, ever so slightly, but altered. Doctor George Gordon had been most sympathetic and attentive in his solicitations. He told Isabella that he understood her feelings and that he knew she was well-nigh inconsolable. He felt the loss keenly himself for James Clark had been his most congenial friend.

THE LADY ISABELLA

Doctor Gordon would not admit that he had long felt an attachment for Isabella; no, no, his frequent visits were to offer his advice and consolation. The Doctor was of a literary turn and read much poetry; so did Isabella, especially the melodious songs of Robert Burns. One night after his return from the Clark home, George Gordon took pen and paper and wrote the following lines which he presented to Isabella on his next visit as an understanding of her feelings:

> *A solemn gloom all Nature wears*
> *Since I am left alone.*
> *Thy Beauty's spring can't soothe my cares*
> *Nor cease my plaintive moan.*

> *For him who gave this life its charms*
> *Lays silent in the grave*
> *No more to bless these widowed arms*
> *While on this earth I stay.*

> *Oh how unwelcome was that doom*
> *Which bid my pleasure fade*
> *And in the cold and silent tomb*
> *The kindest husband laid.*

> *Your lovely orphan children dear,*
> *Sweet pledges of our love,*
> *I'll guard them with a parent's care*
> *Till we do meet above.*

> *There is for me no earthly rest.*
> *Where shall I comfort find*
> *Since he is gone upon whose breast*
> *My aching head reclined?*

The sad sweetness of those lines (aptly called "The Widow's Ode" by one of her descendants), convinced the Lady Isabella that she needed George's help and a year later she married him. It was a most fortunate marriage. She found comfort for her aching head and heart and a long period of happiness began for both of them.

Doctor Gordon had a kindly charm about him that endeared him to everyone; he was popular, lovable and even-tempered. His stepchildren were devoted to him and later on when there were three children of his own he showed no partiality whatsoever in the granting of favors and privileges. His management and understanding of children are shown in a humorous story of school life. When one of the boys of the household came home from Doctor Sampson's school with a story of punishment in which Doctor Sampson had lost his own temper to the extent of breaking a slate over the boy's head and then commanding the boy to pay for the slate, Doctor Gordon sat down and penciled a note to Doctor Sampson saying, "Dear Doctor Sampson—If I furnish the heads it's nothing but fair that you furnish the slates. G. G."

Doctor Gordon's devotion to Isabella was so apparent that it was said that he was putty in her hands. Certainly, it was a willing subjugation on the Doctor's part and he recognized the truth of his friends' jibes. He would have

THE LADY ISABELLA

stated it more prettily but that would have made the situation none the less true.

Twenty years rolled past. Prosperity and happiness dogged their footsteps. The country grew, the town grew, the children grew. Four sons were grown. One son, Pat Clark, was graduated as a Doctor; another one, James, was ready to follow the same medical route. Then came a sudden change. Isabella and Doctor Gordon prepared for another war.

They were ardent secessionists; they attended meetings favoring it; they spoke for it whenever possible; they agreed with the ideas of Charles De Morse as expressed in his editorials of *The Northern Standard,* now changed to *The Standard.* Again Isabella contributed clothing and supplies for recruits of Red River County. She sent her husband and three sons to the service of the Confederate States. Dr. Gordon and Dr. Pat Clark were surgeons of the same regiment. Another son, John Gordon, a private in the army, never returned to Texas. He was killed in action.

But the two Doctors came back; so did Captain James Clark who had served with distinction on the staff of Generals Scurry and Waterhouse. Life began another era with the Clark-Gordons.

In the reconstruction days when Texas was torn asunder politically, the Lady Isabella gave another proof of her firmness and convictions. Judge Albert Latimer was a candidate for some judicial office, and his anti-secessionist views were so recent and so strong that there was some opposition to him. A whispering campaign was organized to dispense rumors of Judge Latimer's Union sympathies and war activities. Isabella Gordon stepped into a printing-office one day and saw a big lot of circulars to be distributed through the town.

"Gentlemen, give me those papers. You're not going to send them out. I have known Judge Latimer for many years. I have disagreed with him politically on every question that has come up. I'm against him but I like him personally. He's a splendid gentleman and you're not going to circulate those lies about him."

With one fell swoop she swept the pile of "dodgers" into the folds of her skirt which she had quickly picked up for the purpose. Judge Latimer won his election, and Isabella's leadership remained intact.

Undoubtedly, that leadership is the reason she is so well remembered today in the city she helped to found one hundred and seven years ago. Incident after incident could be told to reveal her contributions to this great Red River Valley, but the reel unwinds. A builder is ever remembered for what he builds. Miss Ibbie, with all her dominance, her peculiarities, her generosity, her sense of humor and her loyalty, was like that. Perhaps the best tribute is the comment of that historian who said, "Nightly hundreds of lips mention her name in prayer."

15

— LICK SKILLET MEN —

This is not a story of an Epicurean frolic staged in the Reconstruction era, for men from the Skillet carried double-barrelled guns and trusted no one. Consequently, this narrative tells of men who were struggling desperately to bridge the gap between an old order and a new when everything they believed in had been lost. It begins on a summer afternoon in a year when chaos reigned supreme throughout the valley. The long shadow of distress touched heavily a point where four counties meet.

* * * * * *

Down the long winding road from McKinney appeared a solitary horseback rider who rested in his saddle and gazed at the unraveling landscape. Bit by bit he distinguished the trees upon the rise that gave the name of Pilot Grove to the settlement nearby; the houses were too far away for him to know which was the drug store of Doctor Kuykendall and which the Moss Hotel and which the residence of the Brewers. All in good time he would be a part of this landscape. He had heard so much about this corner of four counties that he felt he was familiar with it already.

This ex-Lieutenant of the Texas Rangers was not burdened with wealth or possessions. He had traded his Bowie knife for the horse he was leading behind him. His only other assets were the two six-shooters he wore in his belt and the rifle swung round his saddle-horn. After three years of service on the Mexican frontier William D. Hoard was heading east where, as he remembered it, there were people and civilization. This village he was looking at in front of him was thirty or forty years old and might be the kind of place he was searching for to start a money-making business of some sort. That is, if there were any such thing as money—hard money—to be found in this land of despair.

Coming at a slow pace along the road from town was a wagon drawn by two oxen and carrying as load only a huge barrel. The driver walked beside his team as a means of urging them on a little more rapidly. He held the lines loosely in his hands and seemed on the verge of addressing his oxen with a strong peroration when the ex-Lieutenant of the Rangers decided to intervene.

"Just a minute, brother, before you go on with your lambastin'. Is that th' Skillet over yonder?"

"Yep, that's hit. Ye want hit?"

"How close am I to it?"

"Ye're 'bout at th' end o' th' handle, stranger."

The Lieutenant was interested. "That's what

I am, a stranger, brother. Do ye think it'll be a'ginst me if I stop over there for a spell?"

The driver of the ox-wagon leaned on the wheels and studied the man on horseback. "Don't know 'bout that. Th' Skillet ain't much of a place fer a stranger jus' now, lessen ye kin handle a gun. Better ride on."

William Hoard of the Rangers was a long and angular person to judge from the appearance he made on his horse. His legs seemed dangling from a Totem-pole torso. His arms were longer than the sleeves of his dusty shirt yet his hands grasped tenderly and gracefully a six-shooter in his belt.

"Reckon I can do that, Mister. I been practicin' on th' Feds and greasers for four years." The six-shooter came dangerously close to the chin of the ox-driver. "What you got in that barrel, molasses, water or liquor?"

"Straight whiskey."

"For sale?"

"Might be. We got th' Feds camped here an' they got t' have their liquor. So, you can't git none o' this, lessen ye git it at th' Moss Hotel." He started his conversation to the oxen again and tightened his hold on the lines. But the Ranger dismounted.

"Reckon I need a business an' this is it. Mister, you ain't goin' t' th' Moss Hotel. I got a horse here an' another six-shooter's good as this 'un. You need t' do a little travelin' an' I need a little settlin' so how 'bout it?"

"We-l-l, ye kin go into tha' Skillet if ye want

to but if ye git burned ye can't blame me. Ye named th' terms. I take 'em. That other nag o' yours ain't so good but it looks better 'n any I've seen in five years 'roun here. Untie 'im an' gimme that fancy pistol. I'm a gittin' outa here."

He tossed the lines of his plodding team to the Ranger and lost no time in mounting his new horse without saddle and, pushing the six-shooter through his belt, he rode out of sight to the west. Lieutenant Hoard pondered his purchase.

The result of his thinking was that two hours later he tied his oxen and his saddle-horse to the hitching rack in front of Doctor Kuykendall's Drug Store and went in to get acquainted. He hoped it would be more of a renewal of acquaintances, for he had stopped here a week eight years before. Then he had met the Binions, the Brewers, the Hamptons, Doctor Pierce and Doctor Kuykendall. He wondered what war had done to these people. He recognized the portly Doctor washing bottles in a bowl behind a counter. Four or five men were watching the process.

"Howdy, Doc," spoke the angular Ranger. "Jus' dropped in to see if you was still at th' ol' stand. Had a hankerin' t' find out if ye'd remember me." The thumping of his boot heels made enough noise to attract the ears of all the men and the sight of him now with his right hand resting easily but firmly upon the handle of the six-shooter which protruded from his pants pocket caused them to give him respectful attention.

"Reckon I do, William, reckon I do." The Doctor stopped his washing and reached a hand across the counter. "Where you been, an' where you headin'?"

"Right here," answered the Ranger while his hand slipped back to its pocket rest. "I hear ye got th' Military here and things apt to be lively with that aroun'; business, too. They'll need liquor, won't they? Th' more th' better, an' I got it fer 'em. Well, where's Doctor Pierce?"

There was a silence, broken finally by the druggist. "Well, he jus' ain't here any more, William. We got a new Doctor now, fresh from Mississippi—Doctor Holmes."

The Lieutenant suspected there was more to this item than Doctor Kuykendall chose to tell him. "Forgot t' mention where I'd been when ye asked me. Been with the Rangers three or four years down on th' frontier o' South Texas and the Mexican side too. Pretty bad there. So I dropped back here to see if this part of the state was any better. I kinder liked it here before an' now I think I'll stay. Got to see 'bout puttin' up my business, gentl'm'n, so I'll get on up t' th' Moss Hotel in time for supper. I'll be roun'. Until then, as we say on the border, *adios.*"

However, when he came out of the drug store and untied his oxen he looked at them with misgiving and mumbled in their ears, "I'll be damned if I know what to do with you. Looks like I'd bought myself a white elephant." He guided his equipage up the street to the Moss Hotel, a distance of about three hundred yards. He didn't dare let the barrel of liquor get out of his sight for long. He expected it to be the basis of his business. He tied his team the second time to the center post of the Moss Hotel's front porch and looked up to see a man whom he supposed to be the proprietor standing in the doorway, watching him.

"Good evenin', pardner. Got any supper for a newcomer?"

"Not a mite, sir, not a mite. You're in th' Skillet, ye know, an' they dun cleaned it, ever' smidgeon. But come in, come in; might be some'p'n t' drink."

The Ranger did go in as far as the bar and while he drank he listened to the talk of the men around him. The proprietor was Steve Stephenson and he made a blanket introduction of the Lieutenant as soon as he himself discovered the newcomer's identity.

"We got a Loot o' th' Rangers with us, boys, an' he's come t' stay; if he likes us here."

There were five men sitting together at a table whom Steve introduced with a merry "meet th' Majors—all five of 'em!" And there was a Captain of the Federal forces in his blue uniform who received a casual "that's Captain Robinson, Loot." There was Doctor Holmes— "our new Doc—"—a short slender fellow with keen, dark eyes that held a twinkle. There were probably a dozen others who were residents, sturdy, square-set fellows with beards, also with boots and pistols. Lieutenant Hoard soon decided that here was the place he wanted to stay, with only his white elephant outside to stake him. "By George," he said to himself, "that's what I'll call my place—The White Elephant Saloon." He was so pleased with his new idea that he decided it was worth a treat. He spoke aloud as he flipped a gold coin on the bar to Steve.

"What'll you have, gentl'm'n? Th' drinks are on me. Later on, I hope to sell you all you want, but now it's free."

In less than two months he had made his prediction good. The White Elephant Saloon had become a rendezvous for these booted and bearded men of the Skillet, for the ex-officers of the Confederacy, for the officers and men of the victorious and watchful Federals, for bushwhackers, Union Leaguers, robbers and questionable passers-by. The proprietor of the new spot was doing so well that he was contemplating the installation of a race-course. He had traded his oxen for a fast-stepping horse and he was making plans to acquire others. His initial trade proved to be a lucky change for him. His ears were always open; through them he learned the habits, the customs and the resources of his customers.

The five Majors often met at the Elephant and chatted with him over their drinks. There was Major Thrift, a tall, distinguished Virginian who had served with the Armies east of the Mississippi; Major Levy, a decided contrast in appearance—short, dark and loquacious; Major Sivells, Major Stuart and Major Stinnett, Texans all, with outstanding war records. They were young men, too, who were caught in the maelstrom of economic confusion and as yet had found no method of surmounting it. From them William Hoard heard the tragic story of Bob Lee, the man for whom a thousand dollars reward was offered.

"You see," said Major Stinnett, "Bob was a Captain with Forrest in Tennessee. He was a valuable man to Forrest and the Confederacy for four years. He came back here with the idea of being valuable to his state, too. But everything has worked against him. We're here at the point where Grayson, Fannin, Hunt and Collin counties touch; that's why they sometimes call this place the Four Corners. Bob's father owns land in Hunt and Fannin. When Bob come home, folks noticed he wore better clothes than some of them did; finer than they thought he ought t' have; then he was seen to pass some gold pieces around too freely. They began to suspect him and to tell things about him that they created from someone's imagination. That's the way it started, Lieutenant. There's Union sympathizers around here and they call themselves the Union League; some of them just riff-raff that drifted in here and some of them good people under the influence of the bad. It's as dangerous as running the blockade and smuggling goods across the border and the story's not ended. They got Doctor Pierce because he treated Bob Lee for a wound they had given him. You're a fellow to keep your mouth shut, I can see, Lieutenant. Well, you'd better keep on that way. Good habit in times like these."

The Majors departed in haste and almost in apology for their garrulousness. William Hoard watched for Bob Lee. One day he came. He was well protected by his relatives and his followers. He was a very handsome fellow with a genial, likable manner about him. There was a touch of the picturesque too, in the black felt hat he wore, with its brim turned back and a big, black plume stuck through the corded band. The party left the Elephant in safety that day and the proprietor drew his own conclusions which he communicated to no one.

An open feud developed; it spread across the four counties; it splashed the blood of friends and enemies with reckless abandon. There were men like Lewis Peacock and Hugh Hudson who vowed to rid the country of the Lees and fanned the emotions of the Unionists to fever heat. Followers of the Lees practically barricaded themselves in the denseness of Wildcat Thicket, adjacent to the Lee land.

The Lieutenant succeeded in remaining aloof. The months slipped by until a year had gone and he continued to do business with both sides of the factions. The White Elephant and its race-course prospered. William consulted often with J. P. Dumas, the man who owned so much land that he well could be called the Land Baron of the Four Corners. Dumas surveyed land for the State and was paid in land. He also held a beef contract to supply the Federal soldiers with beef. During the conflict he had supplied beef to the garrison of Fort Washita. He knew how to turn every chance into pennies. He told William many incidents of local history; one of them was about the time Steve Stephenson first called the place Lick Skillet—a stranger had asked for food and Steve said "there ain't none; we lick th' skillet here." Dumas also dropped many a hint to William advising caution if he hoped to make his business permanent.

Such cautions were unnecessary. The very fact that William said he'd served three years with the Rangers seemed to establish his standing as a man not to be trifled with lightly. He exhibited his marksmanship when challenged, but in a friendly manner and always upon an inanimate target or upon some passing fowl of the back-yard or fleeing rabbit of the prairie. He qualified as well able to handle his pistols or rifles and he was besought to align himself with one side or the other of the local parties; to speak publicly his ideas about the way things were going. But not the cautious William; he listened attentively and he showed letters from his superior officers in the Rangers attesting his service and ability but he clung tenaciously to the idea that business was his only interest.

He remained unruffled, even when he was

reading avidly Bob Lee's pathetic appeal for justice in the *Bonham News*—"If you will permit me the use of your valuable columns, I would like to give you a true explanation of the Pilot Grove Difficulty. I was raised in this state and enlisted in the Southern Army and fought the best I could until the surrender, when I laid down my arms and returned home to live, as I thought, in peace the balance of my life. How badly I was disappointed you will soon see.

"A short time after my arrival home, I was arrested by a party of men wearing the U. S. uniform and was told that I would be taken to Sherman to stand trial for offences committed during the War—Imagine my dismay when our entire party halted in Chocktaw Bottom, this side of Sherman. I repeatedly begged to be taken to Sherman but they refused and finally after keeping me thirty-six hours virtually a prisoner, I agreed to give them my mule, saddle and bridle, a $20 gold piece I had in my pocket, and signed a note for $2000 in gold payable on demand. They had no pen and used a toothpick for that purpose and for ink they used gunpowder and water, mixing it in my brother's hand. He had come with me when I was arrested. The next day they allowed us to escape, trying to shoot us as we fled. After my arrest I sought to try the civil law on these scoundrels and ever since they have tried to kill me—Dr. Pierce's death is attributed to his kindness in treating me. The civil authorities take no notice of these things—I have tried to procure peace;

I have even tried to buy it with money—I have done every way in the world to be right and be peaceable; still, I am hunted by a squad of U. S. soldiers.—

"I am willing to surrender to any impartial civil authority at any time but I will not give myself up, unarmed, to thieves and robbers.

"I am sorry to take so much of your valuable space but a great many people, even the Military, have no idea of the true origin of all this trouble. I give you the particulars. I remain yours,

"Robert Lee."

When he came to that signature Soldier William of the Rangers forgot his business at the Elephant and recalled his days of hard riding and straight shooting in the service of another Robert Lee. He clipped this letter from the News, folded it and placed it in his pocket lest he forget Lee's statement.

The letter was Lee's last appeal. Not long afterward he was killed; shot from ambush by one who lay hidden in the brush of Wildcat Thicket to shoot the handsome Captain as he was riding from his hide-out. The news traveled fast, William Hoard heard it at the Elephant in the afternoon after the morning shooting. By the next afternoon he had heard the sequel. The man who was said to have fired the fatal shot at Lee was called to his door at the breakfast hour and shot by his own nephew who looked upon his uncle as a traitor. William's business at the White Elephant was heavy for three days

LICK SKILLET MEN

while men sought to escape from grief, to feed their lusts or to arouse their hatreds.

William predicted—but only to himself—that things would never quiet down until there was a settlement with the other side. He pursued the even tenor of his way and accumulated gold pieces for the future.

One day came the news that the man named Peacock had been shot at his home on Desert Creek by three men who hid all night in the overhanging trees waiting for Peacock to come out and pick up stove wood for his breakfast fire. "Lee's murder is avenged," they shouted before they made their get-away through the brush along the creek.

A sudden quiet descended upon the Skillet. The Military was withdrawn. Men talked more freely in the Moss Hotel and lingered more openly at the Elephant. They exchanged family news at Doctor Kuykendall's Drug Store and gossiped about the new Doctor's patients; they dared to laugh about the Doctor's gray horse which he called Bill and said that old Gray Bill was as good as a newspaper to tell them who was sick. There was talk of naming a new settlement Gray Bill in honor of the Doctor's horse.

Then there came the big revival, a camp-meeting in the brush arbor not far from the White Elephant. Many people changed their ways, among them the ex-Lieutenant of the Rangers. William said he'd got religion and he'd sell no more whiskey or liquor of any kind.

He closed the White Elephant, sold the racetrack and set up his new store wherein he sold only "Dry Goods and Gen'l Mdse."

The peace that Southern soldiers dreamed about came at last. Lick Skillet became a quiet little hamlet and its men tame and tractable. Lieutenant William Hoard made a comfortable fortune while its citizens wrested from Agriculture the means commensurate with their desires.

16

— "On the Banks of the Washita" —

Fort Washita was established upon the banks of the Washita in April, 1842, upon recommendation of General Zachary Taylor as a fort of protection for the Five Civilized Tribes who had been granted reservations in that area. Most frontier forts were built as safeguards against the attacks of war-like Indians, but Washita was a safety zone for the civilized Indians against the wild Indians of the Plains. Perhaps the new fort was a conciliation to those emigrant Indians making their way across the Trail of Tears to their new homes in the West; Indians who were loath to leave the lands of their ancestors but who "being ignorant of the laws of the white man cannot understand or obey them—therefore—have determined to sell their country and hunt a new home."

So read the Pontotoc treeaty signed by the Chickasaw Council in 1832. Its sentiment was echoed by the feelings of the Choctaw, Creek, Seminole and Cherokee Nations, and it was for them the United States Government erected Fort Washita. These peaceful Red Men feared the prowling, predatory activities of the Kiowas, Comanches, Apaches and others; they feared also the desperadoes and guerrillas among the whites from the Texas side.

The fort on the Washita was twenty miles north of the border town of Preston and the same from Colbert's Ferry settlement. The Government carried through General Taylor's recommendations in good style. The War Department erected many commodious buildings in the clearing that was four miles square. It became the center for military excursions along the frontier, for Indian parleys and for social gatherings of the garrison and settlers on the Texas side.

This protective arrangement functioned effectively for twenty years. Then when the spring grass was turning green and the braves were preparing for the buffalo hunt, a new foe appeared. Soldiers began leaving Fort Washita as other soldiers were appearing on the south side of the river. It was war of a kind the Indian could not understand. In his own words it was "the white man's war and the red man's woe."

* * * * * *

A flag that had bars instead of stripes had been flying from the flagstaff of the fort for nearly three months when a famous pow-wow of the Chickasaws and Choctaws took place. Two officers, Colonel W. C. Young and Captain Reeves were standing inside the Colonel's quarters at the Fort waiting and watching for the signal that the Indians were approaching. They knew the war dance was to take place; in fact they had been exerting every effort since they had taken over the half-abandoned fort in May to enlist the Indians in the Confederate army. They remembered well that day north of Preston on Chickasaw land when they had assembled with orders to take Fort Washita. They had marched with alacrity and enthusiasm although they had had no uniforms of any kind and their weapons had been knives, hoes, hatchets and a few rifles and pistols. When they reached the fort full of the war-spirit, even as they were expecting the Indians now gathering on the parade ground to be, they found that the Union garrison had withdrawn towards Kansas leaving only a small supply of corn and oats.

This was also the situation at Fort Cobb and Fort Arbuckle, similar forts and both in the Chickasaw Nation. There were some four hundred men in Fort Washita now who would quickly challenge any attempt of Federal troops to take it. They were in good quarters; there was plenty of food and they were learning military tactics through drilling twice daily. There were over one thousand men doing the same thing along the river's shores—sentinels of the border. It was three hundred miles to Fort Leavenworth in Kansas and Fort Gibson would be disputed territory for either side. The Confederates in command of the border forts had resolved to enlist several companies for the South.

A sound of drums came to the ears of the Colonel. He turned to Captain Reeves. "They are beating the war drums and you know those drums bring war sorter close to us; makes me wonder about a battlefield. What would we do and how?"

An orderly entered the room and stood at attention. "The men are coming into the fort, Sir."

"Well, Captain, let's step out and see how they recruit their men. I sent a letter to the Clarksville paper to raise my companies." They looked at the gathering crowd of Indians. "H'm, quite a crowd here. These are all Choctaws and Chickasaws, you know; women and children are, following after them I see. We may get enough men here to send a company to Ben McCulloch and General Pike."

In preparation for the war dance the warriors were stripped to fighting costume; they were preceded by a drummer and an old chieftain who was evidently to speak. Two others carried the Confederate flag; they stuck the staff securely in the ground and the warriors marched round it in a circle. The beating drum stopped and the old chief stepped forward and spoke.

"Nearly thirty years ago, my brothers, Washington put us on the white man's road. We wanted to go on that road but now the white man is fighting. They have told us not to fight but now our white friends are fighting each other. My people are grieved at this and our heads are cast down in shame." Then with a quick change and a noiseless step the old man began walking round the circle, looking into the faces of the warriors. He raised his voice; his eyes looked upward to the tree-tops as he cried. "Warriors of the Choctaw and Chickasaw Nations! Look round you! What do you see? You see men equipped for war. A strange sight for my young men who have been following the paths of peace! But who are these men? They are the sons of the South who come from the land of sunshine across the river. Men who are in our hearts as their star is in our colors; men, with whom you, my warriors, are to share the glory and the toils of war. You must let the enemy feel the edges of your knives. Let not your warpath be through your own green corn fields but let your knives drink the life blood of your enemies in their own towns and stand side by side with your white brothers who are fighting for their rights and their property, their wives and children. Warriors! We have the same feelings, the same kind of property; look around you and see the women and children of your race who have assembled to see the warriors in their war paint. Their hands have adorned you for the battle and their hearts will be with you on the field of death!"

His voice had gradually grown faster as he spoke; so had his step. Now every warrior had begun to move, round the circle, faster and faster; the drums took the rhythm. The women moved closer toward the circle and began humming a plaintive song; louder and louder grew their song until they ran into the middle of the circle and danced around the flag staff while the men uttered yells of defiance. Then the old chief stepped into the circle and after a mournful wail he spoke above the babble.

"This is the first time some of us have danced in the warrior's line but let not your hearts fail nor your arms grow weak, my brothers! Your country may need every blow!"

The four companies of Confederates who guarded the fort for the Indians were ranged around the parade ground watching this stirring spectacle with confused feelings. Finally Captain Reeves spoke quietly in the ear of Colonel Young.

"No one could beat men who go into battle like that."

"Yet I wonder if we know what we are doing, out here on the western fringe of our Confederacy. That old Chief's words give me a queer feeling in the pit of my stomach. But bring them in and sign 'em up, Captain, when they finish."

There was probably not an officer nor enlisted man who did not share the feeling of the Colonel. They were to remember for many moons the war dance beside the Washita; a dance which resulted in many recruits for the Indian regiments desired by Captain McCulloch, Commander of the Military District of the Indian Territory.

Two months later Captain Albert Pike who had been commissioned Special Commissioner of the Indians held special conferences with the Five Tribes. He negotiated treaties of Alliance with each of the tribes and from them secured his regiments for the Southern Cause. While he was busily engaged in organizing and drilling his new army, the winter months slipped by spreading distress and suffering among the Indian refugees in Kansas and others who had fled to the hills from they knew not what.

But the Choctaws and the Chickasaws who lived beside the Washita were steadfast in their loyalty to the Sons of the South about whom they had chanted in their dance. When spring came round again, Colonel Young received orders to have his troops in readiness to march to Arkansas. Stand Watie of the Cherokees had been made a Colonel and exerted every influence to bring in a few recalcitrant Cherokees who did not accept the treaty of Alliance. Colonel Young was informed that there were only seventeen men in the Choctaw Nation who had not enlisted.

There was much beating of the drums and wailing of the women the day the men marched away to Arkansas with General Pike to fight with Generals Price and McCulloch. This was repeated when the report came in of the defeat of their army at Pea Ridge and the loss of their commander, Ben McCulloch. The Stars and Bars hung at half mast at the fort and the soldiers in the garrison were sad. The old chiefs and the women who came to ask about it could not understand the explanation given them. They could not comprehend defeat in the white man's manner.

The Texas Road between Fort Washita, Boggy Depot and Fort Gibson became disputed ground. Efforts were made by both sides to cut supply trains that were endeavoring to get through to Confederates and to Union men as well. There were the stories of Honey Springs and Cabin Creek and Poison Creek. There was hunger and suffering among the Caddos, the Wacos, and the Wichitas who had fled to the agencies in Kansas. They could not till their lands beside the Washita. Many of them died along the road to Leavenworth. But all that time J. P. Dumas was supplying good meat to Fort Washita at 8 and 10 cents per pound. He lived at Pilot Grove in Grayson County on the Texas side and held a government contract with the Confederacy.

While the soldiers at the fort were feasting on meat, particularly on good buffalo meat, the Indians' supplies grew scantier. One day the old chief who had incited the men to seek blood in the war dance watched with misgiving the unloading of the meat. At length he spoke to Dumas and his boys.

"A long time ago this land belonged to our fathers but when I go up the Washita now I see soldiers on its banks. These soldiers cut my timber and kill my buffalo. When I see that, my heart is sorry."

There were numerous predatory bands who killed the buffalo for sport and left their carcasses where they fell. Then there were the skinners shipping hides where they could; all in all the old chief and others of his tribe saw the buffalo who had furnished them with food, shelter and clothing, rapidly disappearing. Added to that, their stock for farming was driven off or stolen and their feed crops confiscated.

The end of the war was apparent for some months before it became a fact. The border forts prepared for evacuation and surrender while the Indians made a pathetic appeal for a peace council with the Indians of the Plains who once had been their enemies; many of their men had enlisted and returned, some deserted and joined the Union side and others had become roving prowlers and followers of the bushwhackers.

The two principal chiefs of the Choctaw and Chickasaw Nations, Peter P. Pitchlynn and Winchester Colbert, were anxious to unify their people and secure for them the rights and privileges to begin again in the white man's way— rebuild what they had torn down. They called a peace Council of the Five Tribes and the Plains Tribes.

The meeting took place on the banks of the Washita on May 25th, 1865, at a spot they called Camp Napoleon. There's an ironical touch to the choice of name for the pow-wow of a people seeking peace. There, in solemn conclave, and near to the fort that had been built to protect them, they signed a peace pact which said among other things—"Whereas, the history of the past admonishes the red man that his once great and powerful race is rapidly passing away like snow beneath the summer sun and their vast and lovely country and beautiful hunting grounds is now, on account of war and discord, being hemmed into a small and precarious country that we can scarcely call our own, we, the Confederate Indian Tribes and allies of the Confederate States and our brothers of the Plains, do enter into the following compact:

"Peace and friendship shall exist between us—the friendly smoke of our council fires shall ascend to the spirit land to invoke the blessing of the Great Spirit. The tomahawk shall be buried and the scalping knife shall be broken. The path of peace shall be opened from one tribe to another. The motto of the confederated Indian tribes shall be—'An Indian shall not spill an Indian's blood.'

"In testimony whereof we have smoked the pipe of peace and extended to each other the hand of friendship—."

Their peace pact like most of their kind, was not far-reaching, but the peace and friendship they so desired returned to the Washita that same spring. The Confederate garrison withdrew and surrendered their arms and no more soldiers of any sort came to take their places. The buildings and the spacious parade grounds were abandoned to the Indians, perhaps to be used for some future peace parleys and powwows. The smoke of the campfires drifted upwards, and the Indians of the Plains were far away. There were only cattle thieves and desperadoes along the Washita.

17

THE HOUSE OF THE SCREAMING PEACOCKS

Would you care for a dish of fried peacock for breakfast? Perhaps with broiled wild turkey and venison steak on the side? Those are the delicacies you would have been served at Glen Eden in Coffee's Bend one hundred years ago by the prosperous owner, Colonel Holland Coffee, and his charming young wife, Sofia. Peafowls in the wilderness of the Red River country were most unusual and that was likely one reason the Colonel wanted them—he aspired to the unusual, the munificent, the comfortable.

Old-timers in the valley today say their folks told them about the peafowls many times. One of them voiced the concerted opinion: "My father used to go there lots; he said they had five hundred peafowls, all screaming at once when he rode up to the doorway, under them catalpa trees."

The beauty of the catalpa trees, and the commotion of the peacocks impressed every traveler who dilly-dallied at the hospitable river mansion. Travelers were frequent one hundred years ago; and if they came, they dilly-dallied. No eat-and-run methods were known or dreamed about. It was not a case of grab your bag and *vamoose* but bring your baggage and stay. Each new landholder building his home in the valley was anxious that his place should be known for its hospitality, its refuge and protection from dangers, its good food with enjoyment of it for all who cared to partake of it.

Colonel Holland Coffee had those ideas and qualities in mind when he built his home in Coffee's Bend for his promised bride. He had land—hundreds of acres of it in his own headright and he knew people—all kinds of people—for many miles on both sides of the river. From Fort Gibson to San Antonio he knew Choctaws, Chickasaws, Cherokees, Kiowas, Comanches, Osages, hunters, trappers, soldiers, farmers, colonizers and politicians—from the Chief of the Cherokees to the President of the Republic at Austin.

Regarding the last named personage, Holland Coffee had met Sam Houston in 1832 at Fort Gibson when the dark-skinned Tennesseean was sojourning with the Indians. After that he made a republic and became the president of it. At Fort Gibson, Coffee had talked with many people making their way to Texas. In 1834 he followed them but only as far as the Red River. His intuitive business sense told him that here was opportunity for trade that could not be surpassed at any point in the new country. He chose a bend in the river and established Coffee's Station or Coffee's Bend; whichever name you used, your path would soon have led you to the trading post. Situated on the main north and south road for settlers and within one day's riding from almost any point of the "Trail of Tears" it really was a meeting point of the two races. Indian and white man bargained with the Colonel (we've never found when, where or why he acquired that title) for furs, for beads, for food and clothes.

Colonel Coffee was a linguist of no mean ability, and though he was not a globe trotter who jumped from world capital to world capital, he conversed fluently and understandingly in seven dialects of the Indians. Add that to his English-speaking habits and you have eight languages chalked up to the credit of the river trader and adventurer. He made his knowledge of vocabularies react to his own financial advantage which is more than many a modern linguistic artist can do.

Coffee's path crossed Houston's again in 1837 at Washington-on-the-Brazos. The Colonel was there for his wedding to Sofia Suttonfield, the daughter of an army officer stationed at Fort Wayne, Indiana. The bride was only twenty and well advanced in charm for she had already broken the heart of a husband and touched with ambition the hearts of many men. But the shrewd trader from the Red River country had a way with him too, and it was he who led the saucy little Sofia to the altar.

In the festivities celebrating the wedding there was dancing, and President Houston of the well-established republic of Texas danced with the bride and bade her bon voyage on her honeymoon trip to her new home on the northern frontier. He informed her that her husband's trading station was not far from the haunts of his Indian brothers, the Cherokees, and of other Indians friendly to the white man and promised to visit the new home when completed.

The bride and groom then set out on horseback for their six-hundred-mile cross-country trip but history does not record the time log of the voyage. They finally reached the home of Daniel Montague in Grayson County, and there a grand welcoming ball was given.

Colonel Coffee had begun the erection of his own home but it was not yet completed when he arrived at the Montagues with Sofia. Consequently she remained at the Montagues until she could give a welcoming party herself and initiate a series of social good times that should extend through the years, thereby building an enviable reputation for the girl from Fort Wayne. Her first appearance as hostess was at the house-warming of her new home. The affair lasted more than two days, for there was no hurry and skurry about the parties in 1840. There were hundreds of guests at this affair, some of them coming from as far as Austin to the south, Jefferson to the east and Fort Gibson to the north.

What a note of happiness is indicated in the choice of the name Glen Eden; Glen it most certainly was topographically for it was en-

HOUSE OF SCREAMING PEACOCKS

closed by the bend of the river and by oak and pecan trees. To those who christened it the house was truly a haven of happiness. It was built according to the frontier rules of architecture—a double log cabin with open hall. Later there was added the ell with kitchen, dining-room and cellar. Another luxurious note was added by the six fireplaces. The Colonel was determined to be comfortable in cool weather, so he built the fireplaces; he bought the slaves, and he was surrounded by firewood to be had for the cutting.

Good food was another characteristic of the place that was evident from the first. The Colonel had beef cattle and yearlings in the corral, some fat pigs in a log pen, and there was plenty of wild game on every side of them. If his palate craved turkey, venison or buffalo he had simply to send a hand or to go himself a very short distance into the woods with a gun and return with the desired delicacy.

If his slaves—his cooks, his body servants or his field-hands—became unsatisfactory in any way, he had simply to trade or sell them at his trading post. There he came in contact with almost every sort of person and merchandise. It was an easy matter to acquire comforts and luxuries as he pleased. He wanted his pretty young wife Sofia to have fine clothes and she had them. At the housewarming she is said to have been the envy of every woman in the valley.

President Houston kept his promise and arrived at the new home on Red River in time for the party. He was another person who never minded arduous trips if they ended at pleasing spots. This one, perhaps he thought, might bring a renewal of old friendships of Fort Gibson, a meeting with some who might have known his Indian wife, Diana Rogers. Yet he loved the country to the south and foresaw vast possibilities for it. He longed to bring a closer union with the frontier.

"My dear Sofia," he said in greeting. "I have brought you something for your new home which I hope will last through the years. It will serve to remind you of the central part of our great state and your sojourn at Washington-on-the-Brazos. Its blossoms are as soft and sweet as the breezes that sweep inward from the Gulf on summer evenings. I could think of nothing better than a magnolia tree for your front yard." He turned to his body servants. "Fetch in that young tree, boys, for Mrs. Coffee to look at and then take it out to the smoke-house for the time being."

The President's gift out-lasted all others for there it stands today, tall, stately, magnificent, in the front yard of Glen Eden bespeaking a welcome to every visitor. The world has changed greatly since President Houston made his presentation speech, but the magnolia tree still sheds its perfumed blossoms, even as he said.

Trees, flowers and shrubs of all kinds were sought with eagerness by the homebuilders of the 1840's. They wanted their yards to show

HOUSE OF SCREAMING PEACOCKS

their home-making qualities as plainly as did their kitchens or their parlors.

There came another visitor to Glen Eden a little later who noted the increasing beauty of Houston's tree and the admiration of his hostess for it. He put it upon his mind to bring her some odd tree or flower when opportunity afforded. He was a young army officer stationed at the new Fort Washita, twenty miles north of Glen Eden on the northern side of the river.

When subsequently he was ordered on a trip to California, he remembered Mrs. Coffee of Glen Eden who liked trees and flowers. He purchased and took back with him the seed of some catalpa trees whose white blossoms had fascinated him greatly. Soon after his return to Fort Washita he was invited to Glen Eden. In company with other officers he made the trip, taking the catalpa seeds with him. In after years twenty-four of these "trees of Paradise" bordered the driveway from the road to the house. In the spring of the year their fragrance was like incense and created a nostalgic and lasting impression to incoming and outgoing guests. The donor of the trees was the hero of Shiloh— Albert Sidney Johnston.

The catalpas, the magnolia, and the peacocks were the most conspicuous touches of beauty and color surrounding the house. Just when the iridescent birds were added is uncertain. Whether introduced by some guest, by Colonel Coffee or his wife is unknown. Whoever it was, showed a characteristic which seemed to be typical of the Colonel—the love of the unusual. A flock of several hundred peafowls was maintained for years.

General U. S. Grant and General Robert E. Lee were once members of the Sixth Cavalry while it was stationed at Fort Washita. They were young West Pointers then and were among those who galloped the twenty miles to attend parties at Glen Eden. Many well-known army officers who later became embroiled in the War Between the States had at least most pleasant recollections of the house on Red River. Jesse James and Quantrell's Men took quarters there also when they became the guerrillas of the valley.

Glen Eden's happiness was shattered for a time when Holland Coffee, linguist and trader, merchant and builder, was fatally wounded by one of his customers. In an argument with an Indian he was stabbed in the back and died there among his trinkets and beads, his calico and cattle. It seems a little ironical that Coffee who prided himself upon his ability to understand the Indian and who for so long held the confidence and friendship of so many red men should die at the hand of one of them.

The Colonel's wife, Sofia, had a brick mausoleum built in the new orchard of Glen Eden and there she enshrined the body of her husband. She planted a grapevine above it to climb gracefully about the brick. You may go to Glen Eden today and see the red brick vault and the clinging grapevine. Both look astonishingly

HOUSE OF SCREAMING PEACOCKS

young when you consider that it has been almost one hundred years since they were put there. It seems likely now that they will be disturbed soon, for Glen Eden's site lies within the Red River Dam condemned area. The Coffee pile of brick is valueless.

The catalpas—fragrant "trees of Heaven"—have disappeared and the screaming peafowls are no longer there to shout and strut and preen, but the house still looks serenely toward the road and Sam Houston's magnolia waits expectantly for the admiration of another guest. There is quiet around the house except for the distant hum of motor cars and the scream of sirens. Then a shriek comes closer as a car turns in. You're a tourist and a sight-seer though, not a guest.

> Come see a mansion on the river's bluff
> That speaks of a vanished day
> When white men carved life from the rough
> And red men passed this way;
>
> Where Indian traded captive white
> For liquor, jewels, gold
> To a Colonel who understood
> The heart of the primitive soul.
>
> Here President Houston came to a ball
> And brought his gift with him—
> A gift as soft as his hostess' shawl—
> Magnolia blooms for the river's rim.
>
> Yes, men of great celebrity
> Have stopped at Glen Eden's door;
> Men like Johnston, Grant and Lee—
> They made and they loved its lore.

18

— LOOM OF DESTINY —

Strange are the patterns of the Master-Weaver! Fascinating are the effects achieved! With uncanny skill He reaches over the mountains, across an ocean or a continent to choose materials which will give vivid and permanent hues of beauty. It happened that way once, over in Clarksville in the 1860's.

In the early 1830's an Indian trader and freighter passed through Clarksville. He was from Santa Fe, New Mexico, and was acting as guide to a party of travelers en route to Fort Parker, Texas. Obviously he liked the Red River country for when he returned to the ancient city of the Holy Faith and the near-by Indian village of Taos, where he also went often to trade, he made arrangements to take his family to the valley of the Caddos, the plains of the Rio Roxo of the Spanish. In 1839 he arrived to cast his lot with the people in this wooded, fertile valley. Perhaps the secluded peace of its woods appealed to him after the high mountains and plateaus of New Mexico. At any rate he dropped from an altitude of 7000 feet to a low of 500 feet and liked it. He watched the immigrants streaming into the new republic. He saw a big opportunity for trade with little competition. He established the Donoho Hotel. The man was James Donoho.

However, he did not long enjoy the anticipated pleasures of life in Texas, for he died in 1845, only six years after he had come to Clarksville. But in that time he had sketched the pattern of life for his family. His wife was a strong and fearless woman, intelligent and practical as well; so were his daughters. They were cut by the pioneer pattern. The only boy of the family and namesake of his father thought the hotel was a lot of fun. He was two when they left New Mexico. Now he was eight, big enough to talk to the stage drivers who came in the hotel and to watch the wagons in the Square.

Five thousand miles away at this same time —the middle 1840's—an English family sailed from England for Canada. They were devout Methodists and longed to spread the doctrines of John Wesley. The father envisioned himself and his sons as missionaries in the new country. His wife shared his zeal and ambition but like every mother she also dreamed for her daughter a life that would be better than hers—education, position and other opportunities that could not be gained in their old environment.

They left their home in Shrewsbury with high purpose and ideals. That is, the grown-ups did; the little girl in the party left with tears in her eyes because she had to leave her playhouse in the garden. She wondered if she would ever have another one as pretty.

Jimmy Donoho grew up in Clarksville, pampered by five sisters and his mother. He had a charm about him that helped to make the hotel popular. When he was twenty-three he joined the 29th Texas Cavalry then being recruited for the southern Confederacy by Captain Charles De Morse, editor of *The Northern Standard* of Clarksville. For nearly four years he was absent from the Red River County capital while his mother and sisters carried on the business at the hotel.

Their business was good at the large, two-storied, two-verandahed establishment on the northwest corner of the Square. There was a thick row of trees in front of the hotel which provided a cool shade for the morning sun, and heat and dust protection in the long summers. Another feature that was familiar to every Clarksvillian and every traveler who visited there more than once, was a huge iron bell mounted on a thirty-foot pole just outside the entrance. The bell served many purposes, the most popular of which was its loud sonorous call to meals when Mrs. Donoho gave the signal to pull the cord. When Jimmy came home on furloughs from the war there were often extra clangings of the bell. Additional meals were served to Jimmy and the soldiers and officers he drew there with him, likewise in Texas on furlough.

It was on just such a furlough that Jimmy and his friends heard about a camp-meeting at Coleman's Springs then being conducted by the

Reverend J. W. P. MacKenzie. Jimmy's friends at supper that night were not only men in uniform but men and boys of the community—members of the Home Guard, boys of the Square and the country. Jimmy was told that Mrs. Gordon had taken a group of young ladies to the camp-meeting. Being Irish and fond of a joke, Jimmy conceived the idea of a surprise attack on the camp-meeting, and more particularly upon Mrs. Gordon's party of young ladies.

"Begorra an' I thought things wuz mighty lonesome roun' here," said Jimmy. "Boys, le's go t' meetin'."

The suggestion was pleasing to the eight or ten men who could get horses to ride. The camp-meeting was ten or twelve miles out from town but that meant nothing to young men who had been making forced marches of twenty to thirty miles a day through terrain far worse than the sandy lanes of Red River County. It was so late at night when the boys reached Coleman's Springs that they staked their horses and dropped upon the sand to catch a few winks before observing the next day's activities at the meeting.

Jimmy Donoho and his companions awoke to look over the camp and ponder some way to gain the attention of the girls in Mrs. Gordon's care. In the light of day when they saw Miss Ibbie and her girls and other feminine campers stepping decorously toward the morning service, the boys got the big idea. They found Miss

Ibbie's tent and knowing the ladies to be absent they boldly looked inside. The first sight that greeted them was an array of hats—ladies' hats of varied sorts and sizes. "How about it, boys?" asked Jimmy with a twinkle. "Think this might help?"

His words were no sooner said then the expected action took place. The boys grabbed up all the hats they saw and took them and cached them in a secure place. Then they waited developments.

The Reverend MacKenzie noted the presence of some new faces in his afternoon audience. He spoke of his pleasure in seeing army boys faithful to their religious duties. Then he made an announcement that a number of hats had been taken from Mrs. Gordon's tent; either that, or the young ladies had forgotten where they had left their hats. He trusted that whoever found them would notify him or return them to their owners, if they knew the hats that well. Jimmy and his friends listened attentively to the preacher's words.

The young men appeared again at the evening service. They occupied one of the rear benches and were observed to indulge in a good many pleasing whispers to each other. Just after the singing of "Amazing Grace" the Reverend MacKenzie gave the same announcmeent about the hats but in a much sterner voice this time. Jimmy Donoho stood up.

"Brother MacKenzie, I beg to report that my comrades and I have been in search of those hats. We were determined that they should be found! and they *have* been found. One of th' boys is guardin' 'em outside th' arbor here. Th' owners can have 'em right after th' meetin's over if they'll come an' claim 'em."

The Reverend MacKenzie had a difficult time after that in holding the attention of his audience but he manfully stuck to his subject; he even elaborated upon it for an extra twenty minutes as an expression of his belief in it. When he did pronounce the benediction, there was a scramble and a chatter. The entire assembly moved out to watch the exchange of hats.

Jimmy Donoho picked up the first hat he saw and turned to face a serious-eyed young lady. She didn't speak, so Jimmy did.

"Is this your hat, Miss, or Ma'am?"

"Miss, if you please. Miss Davies, Ellen Davies. And it *is* my hat. Why did you take it?"

"Well, you see, Miss Davies, we didn't— that is—we didn't mean anything. Just a little fun. You see, don't you?"

"Perhaps. But please handle my hat carefully. I brought it with me from Canada and goodness knows when I shall ever have another one."

Jimmy glanced briefly at the little piece of straw and ribbon and handed it to her quickly. He was stunned by that one word *Canada*.

"Did you say Canada? Can any woman in Texas afford to import hats from Canada? Excuse me, but are you—?"

"A refugee? Assuredly; for the same reason that the hats can't get in I can't get out—the blockade. Therefore you will see that I must guard my one hat carefully. Thank you and good evening, Mr. Donoho."

She moved away but Jimmy moved also. All the hats had been re-claimed and the crowd was thinning rapidly. Only a few couples, and stragglers remained near the brush arbor.

"I think you need a military escort to Miss Ibbie's tent, Miss Davies, and I am very glad to be assigned to that duty." He glimpsed a frown upon her face. "No use to object; I haven't got my say out. How did you know my name? You wasn't here on my last furlough. At least I hope not. I'd hate to think I neglected my duty toward the girls of Red River County. Now who told you?"

"Mrs. Gordon told me all about you. Well, that is, she told all her girls about all of you after the morning service. If I may say so, Mr. Donoho, you must be Irish for you have the gift of gab."

"Sure an' my father was a trader on th' Santa Fe Trail. He never saw a stranger and neither do I. But suppose you do th' talkin' for awhile. Tell me when you came and—"

"And why, I suppose. Since you must know and will find out anyway, I'll tell you. I've been in Clarksville only three months. I came with my friends, the Cheathams. Things got so bad in Louisiana that they decided to take what they had and come over here. They invited me to come with them and I accepted. My brother had been sent to New Orleans, after I had come all the way from Toronto to visit him, and on account of the blockade I couldn't go back. So you see, I am very far from my home and family."

"Well, I'll be damned, excuse me, Miss Davies, I'll be—oh, gosh a-mighty! Ellen, that's tough luck for anybody, much less for somebody like you. But we'll make it up to you here in Texas." He glanced ahead of them at a chattering group of girls beside a tent and then lowered his voice. "There's your outfit waitin' for you. I see Miss Ibbie buzzin' roun' out there, but for reasons unknown to you I don't want t' get in an argument with *her* tonight." He took a step or two and then returned. "Oh, by th' way I'm pow'ful ignorant about Canada but anxious to learn. I don't even know what part of Canada that hat come from, nor that accent either, but there's one thing I *do* know—I like 'em both. Good night, Ellen."

Jimmy disappeared in the darkness to find his comrades. He hadn't wanted to meet Mrs. Gordon because he knew she would see through the subterfuge of the hats and after his talk with Ellen it didn't seem as funny as it had. He wanted to explain to Mrs. Gordon, but not here with her party of girls. He would wait until she returned to town from the campmeeting. He felt cheated that neither she nor anyone else had told him about the Cheathams from Louisiana. His mother and sisters would surely know about this girl from Canada.

She had such a sad expression and her eyes were so direct they were puzzling. He had never met an independent female, alone, unprotected, but capable. Could she be like that? No, most likely she was in distress about something and needed somebody to help her out. There was one thing—he had a few more days of furlough and time a-plenty. Perhaps he could help her. He had five sisters and he knew he'd hate to think of any one of them away in a foreign country among strangers.

Sleep deserted him that night. The other boys soon were snoring but he lay and looked at the stars and wondered about the strangeness of meeting a girl from Canada at a camp-meeting in Clarksville.

When he returned to town the next day, he lost no time in getting the story of Ellen Davies. From his mother, his sisters and his friends he asked questions and more questions until he was satisfied that he could hear no more except from the young lady herself. It was a captivating story and quite surpassed any that he had heard in war time. She was an English girl who had come to Canada when she was four years old. Her family had settled in the city of Toronto where her father and two brothers had become preachers of the Methodist church. She had received her education in the best schools and colleges of Toronto but there was evidently a love for travel implanted in her nature for when one of her brothers was sent as a missionary to Louisiana in the States she expressed a great desire to visit him in that far-away South. She gained her wish and set out alone when she was nineteen. Coming by boat from New York to New Orleans she was met by her brother and taken to his station in Southwestern Louisiana. His district lay in the parishes wherein were situated the cities of Shreveport and Alexandria. There she had been caught in the drag-net of war.

Ellen Davies found herself an alien in a foreign land, a friendly land but also a determined, fighting land. She had had no idea of war and had paid little attention to the developing crisis in the States. The routine of her life was changed overnight; the cobweb of her dreams was destroyed. She discovered that she could not return to her parents' home in Canada; the blockade had set in. Soon she could not get letters through. She was completely encircled by a war which she did not understand.

She made new friends and entered into the activities of war work with the women of Shreveport. Her brother was away in army camps and hospitals, finally writing her from New Orleans that he did not know when he would be able to return to Shreveport and advising her to rely upon the advice of his friends, the Cheathams.

Jimmy's friends in Clarksville told him that the Cheathams were well-liked and that they would likely stay for the duration of the war if not permanently. For they said, "Good crops can be made here and land is cheap, which is more that you say for Shreveport for awhile." Miss Ellen Davies had been "stand-offish" at first or at least they thought so, but now she was "thawing out" and popular with all the young ladies of the town and especially with Mrs. Gordon. Jimmy's mother and sisters summed it up for him.

"Jimmy boy, we don't know just what she's like yet but we're goin' to find out. They say she's had lots o' schoolin' an' we're goin' to give her a chance to use it. She's goin' to teach a school here in Clarksville come September. We can tell you more next time, Jimmy."

Jimmy went to Mrs. Gordon's one evening in the hope that Ellen Davies would be there. Mrs. Gordon always entertained for the soldiers at home on leave. There was a crowd of people and dancing and good food, but the English girl was absent. Jimmy cornered his hostess in protest.

"Miss Ibbie," for Mrs. Gordon was Miss Ibbie to every home-town boy, "why isn't that new girl here? I thought you had her under your wing. I've been trying to see her every day since the camp-meetin' and I can't find her. Now, is that kind?"

"She was invited, Jimmy, and may come yet with Mr. and Mrs. Cheatham. In the meantime, look about you, my boy. Gather ye rosebuds while ye may!" She floated away from him on her excess ruffles and attached herself to a lively group of girls and boys. Jimmy followed suit but kept his eyes above the crowd searching for a serious, strange girl.

His Irish luck was with him, for she did appear just before the party ended. Jimmy was at her side in a moment.

"Howdy, Ellen! We been expectin' you."

"Have you, Mr. Donoho? Why?"

"Because I wanted to see you ag'in, that's why. My furlough's up. I haven't been able to find you since that day we met at th' camp-meetin', oh, a long time ago." His eyes twinkled in pleasure as he noted that she was not only serious-eyed and tall but beautiful as well. "Knew you tho', even without your hat. There's dancin' in th' next room. Le's step it with 'em. Come on, there's not much time."

Ellen Davies was charmed with the gay friendliness and hearty enthusiasm of this young man. She did not dance—she never had—but she watched him "stepping it" with other young ladies and decided that he must be a "likeable chap" because he looked so healthy and so light-hearted. Watching him made her forget her troubles for awhile. The evening drew to its merry close. Good-byes were said but Ellen walked home with the Cheathams instead of Jimmy Donoho. She had refused his request. He walked home dejected, and puzzled because he *was* dejected.

* * * * * *

When next they met, the war had ended. Texas men were coming home—mustered out at Hempstead, and at points beyond the Mississippi. More than a year had passed. Ellen was still in Clarksville; she had taught two terms of school. Now she was more serious than ever, for at last a letter had come through from Canada. Both her mother and father had died. She knew now she would never go back. She had lost her home and family in this war; she felt its privations keenly but she had grown to love the Red River Valley country and its people. They became her adopted family.

That lucky Irishman, Jimmy Donoho, came back hale and hearty. His optimism and faith in the future were like sparks of good cheer on the coals of her despair. Ellen found herself welcoming him with a touch of his own enthusiasm. She wondered afterwards at her actions and thought it peculiar but pleasant. She had put sorrow behind her; likewise she cast aside analysis and self-reprimand. Jimmy's flashing smile and cheerfulness gave her confidence as nothing else had since she had come to Texas.

When New Year's Day came round—the new year of 1866—there was a wedding at the Donoho Hotel. Ellen had discovered that a certain contagious confidence was as necessary to her happiness as the sunshine that she breathed. As for Jimmy, he was frank to admit the exigency of a wedding.

"It's bound t' be right, Ellen. I knew it when I met you at th' camp-meetin' but I had t' go back to my soldierin'. Well, that's over, and we can start th' new year together. Sure an' I'm worthless without ye! You steady me an' make me feel I've got t' get somewhere. Ma always told me that too but I wouldn't mind her. But you—well, gosh-amighty, honey, guess you'll have t' teach me th' rest of your life, in all but *one* thing—that's love. Mebbe, I can teach you a little bit there. Turn about's fair play!"

It was a wedding to remember. Jimmy's mother and sisters out-did all past records in preparations and festivities. The friends of the English school-teacher showered her with gifts and convinced her that she had a place in their hearts, just as Jimmy had said she would have. The old bell in front of the hotel rang merrily and often.

The Master-Weaver must have been pleased. Never was a more perfect pattern of happiness woven! Its beauty lasted many years.

19

— "As Long as Water Runs" —

Colbert's Ferry was the best-known of all the ferries across Red River. For over seventy years there was a cable ferry at this point, about four or five miles northeast of the present city of Denison and no more than two miles east of the Government's Red River Dam.

In the days before toll bridges, free bridges, and dams there was so much business at the ferries that camp was made many times by the immigrant wagons while they waited their turns to cross. And the greatest traffic jam of all was at Colbert's Ferry. B. F. Colbert was the ferryman and a shrewd and able one at that. He had no need to worry about competition for his concession was one based on the laws of nature, not of man.

Early in the Fifties Colbert attended a council of the Chickasaws. He himself was a Chickasaw and their land given to them by the United States Government, lay in juxtaposition to the land of the Choctaws—an arrow's flight could bridge the gap. Colbert was not the sort of brave to sit in his wigwam and plot acts of revenge for the coming of the white man; neither did he spend his time in dreaming of the past and making moan for things that used to be. He studied the problem of adjusting himself to the white man's world. He watched the caravans of settlers coming into Texas by the thousands; passing through his country to California and the gold mines, to some Eldorado he did not understand. This much he did know—in their rush to get somewhere they had to cross the river. From the door of his wigwam he watched them and he resolved to acquire some of this gold they were so anxious to find. He saw a way to obtain it right here. But first he would make sure that he would not be pushed aside by the white men in their frenzy or by the red men in their envy. Hence he attended the parley of the Chickasaws.

Here he obtained the thing he wanted—a franchise to operate a ferry across Red River for "as long as grass grows and water runs." That franchise he guarded above everything else in his possession. Well that he did, for soon he began to make money from his ferrying and others saw the opportunity they had missed.

It was a cable ferry, not large, not speedy but it served his purpose through many years. At first only one wagon could cross at a time and the toll money was tossed into a wooden keg, standing near the Indian who pulled the cable. Thousands upon thousands crossed here. The Butterfield Overland stage line, cattle drivers, immigrants and soldiers—all came down the Texas Road and crossed at Colbert's. Desperadoes with their stolen gold crossed back and forth from the Territory to Texas. Before many years B. F. Colbert owned all the land for five miles east and west of his ferry and his franchise was still good with Uncle Sam and with the Chickasaws.

In the early Seventies the coming of the railroads was the most absorbing thought and topic of business and conversation. In Texas a railroad was coming north toward Red River from Austin. It was called the Houston and Texas Central. In the Territory a railroad was coming south toward Red River from Saint Louis. It was called the Missouri, Kansas and Texas. It seemed likely that they would meet at Colbert's Ferry.

The story is told today in Denison—the Katy's gateway city—that the H. & T. C. was so anxious to beat the Katy to Red River that they sought out Ben Colbert and offered him $20,000 for a townsite on the south side of the river at the point opposite his ferry. The Katy's construction had been held up in the Indian Territory due to one of the two great forces, Labor or Capital. In the Katy's case, according to the best reports, it was Capital. Colbert, the shrewd Chickasaw, was not so concerned about the Katy's troubles with capital. His own capital was steadily increasing. He closed the deal for the townsite and carried the $20,000 in currency home to his wigwam. That must have been considered an excellent trophy of the chase. Instead of hanging his trophy or mounting it on a pole he put it in a tin bucket and buried it in his back yard. Then he looked around for *Katy* and the new town across the river.

The new town was to be called Red River City from the little settlement already there. As the story goes it was disappointing to the promoters when the Post Office Department at Washington refused the name because of the well-known cattle crossing in Montague County called Red River Station. And then along came a big rise in the river which washed away all semblance of a town on the low flat shore of the south side. But Colbert still had his twenty thousand hidden away.

Finally the Katy's promoters got over the river and selected a spot on higher ground a mile or two above the Red River City venture. They planned to buy University land from the state but they discovered that a certain B. F. Colbert had already bought a good-sized block of it, for which they quickly paid him $3500. Colbert took that home and added it to his treasure but he did not come to the new town of Denison for three years. This time the business venture succeeded; the town grew and Colbert was underpaid rather than overpaid.

It is said that he kept his $20,000 until the Kansas City Bridge Company persuaded him to enter into partnership with them in building a toll bridge. Since he owned the franchise they considered it better business to take him into the firm than to pay him a huge sum. The bridge was to cost $40,000 and Colbert dug up his $20,000 and went in fifty-fifty with the bridge company. That was 1873 and three years later the river, in one of its sudden and disastrous floods, washed away the whole structure as nothing more than a piece of driftwood in its ever-restless current.

But the franchise read for "as long as water runs." Another and larger cable ferry was soon plying the river again. Colbert's Ferry continued on that steady basis until 1931. One Denisonian says that the Denison Bridge Company's bridge erected in 1920 was sold to the state for $50,000 and that $10,000 was given to the Colberts. Recently there has been some active oil leasing for sites directly in the river's bed not far from Colbert's Ferry. It may be that some day a new kind of gold, one that the first B. F. Colbert never dreamed of, will flow over the ferry site into the hands of the Colbert descendants who may thank their progenitor for his foresight.

There were at least seven other ferries in Grayson County, some of them in operation until the last decade. At the western edge there was Delaware Bend with ferry that was a local for the settlers. A famous murder occurred here in the Eighties when four men were killed by one man in a blacksmith shop near the ferry.

Henderson's and Willis' ferries were useful and popular but never commercial. The next one coming eastward was Rock Bluff and it was second only to Colbert's.

There is a well-known story about a Scotchman who came to work at this ferry in 1870. John Malcolm had started to Mexico City with a friend but at the Red River crossing he stopped to take the job as ferryman at Rock Bluff. He tells in one of his letters that he took a herd of 1800 across one day at Rock Bluff. He says he was a little worried about the problem but the natural chute caused by the rock jutting out into the river was a big help for the cattle could go into the water swimming. But first he and the cattle drivers had to stampede the cattle by yelling and shooting their pistols into the air. Animals of any kind would waste no time in swimming away from that, we imagine. If by accident some of the cattle got to milling in midstream the ferryman had to go out in a skiff and break the mill.

Malcolm also worked at Colbert's Ferry when business was at its peak. Sometimes he put across two hundred wagons per day with the toll receipts running $300. Colbert had to run two ferries for a time. On the south side of the river —the Texas side—there was the store owned by some of the Colberts. That, too, did a big business. It carried groceries, dry goods and whiskey. It was called "First and Last Chance" by some and Red River City by others. When Indians returned to their side of the river they usually needed the assistance of the ferryman— one like the industrious and thrifty Mr. Malcolm.

In about 1875 a new ferry was put into

operation from the Texas side. This too had its take-off from a high rock bluff but it was a little below the Rock Bluff and a little above the Colbert. The ferry business seemed a good bet any time and this ferry continued its runs until about 1936. It wasn't Labor or Capital that stopped it then; it was the river. A sand bar formed in its path and while the river slid round it and went on its way there was no way to get the ferry around it except to go on down to Colbert's and that would not be good business in any man's language, so Baer's Ferry suspended operations. It had been started by Julius Baer, a German with a wooden leg, and was continued by his son for many years. It took the U. S. Government to dislodge the sand bar and now the huge power plants of the Red River Dam occupy the exact spot of the old German's ferry.

Since the Fifties the majority of ferries have been in Grayson County; that is, when we keep to the classification of the valley as the border counties from Cooke to Bowie, including Marion. There is another interesting synonym for that division if we say from Red River Station to Trammel's Trace. The Red River Station crossing and settlement (the same that antedated Red River City) was in Montague County but very near the Cooke County line and much of the cattle driving of the Chisholm Trail crossed at this point. That same Chisholm Trail was split in these two counties, for in Cooke County the Trail crossed at Sivell's Bend.

Fannin County had one or two well-known ferries; one of the oldest in the valley was Sowell's Bluff where later on a toll bridge was erected. The toll-keeper was a woman for many years, but in 1940 the river put a stop to it—not by forming a sand-bar this time but by one of its sudden floods. There was another river crossing in Fannin County that was referred to as the "Whiskey Trail." This title of course dates the crossing as a business venture of the prohibition era. This river crossing in pursuit of liquor is a funny thing—in the early years when the Indians were under the direct supervision of their Uncle Sam they had to come across on the Texas side to get the "fire-water" the white man had brought and in later years when the white man's drinking was under the direct supervision of that same benevolent Uncle he had to cross to the Oklahoma side to buy it from those who had it in hidden caches and "joints" and taverns.

Lamar County's most famous ferry was Fulton's Ferry, north of Paris near a little community called Arthur City. This was a very busy place and was used by many of the earliest settlers coming into Texas during the days of the Republic. But the river closed that business too by changing its course so that Fulton's Ferry was left as a high, dry spot in the sand. This *Riviere Rouge* as the French called it has been very fickle in its dealings with the white man's business ventures.

Trammel's Trace was a very old crossing in

the edge of the present Bowie County. It was used by the Indians; then as a commercial crossing by Nick Trammel, one of the first white men to come to the Red River country. Nature had built a sort of raft that aided the ferrying greatly.

But of all the engineering tricks of Nature none equaled the "Big Raft" on Cypress Bayou. This of course was in Marion County which although not a border county was for many years the heart of the valley because of the port of Jefferson. All water traffic coming into the valley was routed to Jefferson by the way of Red River, Caddo Lake and the Big Raft.

Smaller boats plied the upper Red as far as Red River City and Preston. There were never very many boats and the farther up the river they went, the smaller they became; sometimes they dwindled to canoes, skiffs, flat-boats and keels. As far as Lamar the Sulphur and the North Sulphur were contributing streams and people in Paris used to get their supplies shipped in by water. Sometimes the boats got stranded on sand bars and had to wait for the next rise in the river but eventually they reached their destinations. Possession was more important than the time element then and nobody complained.

"Floating down the river to Shreveport" has been the melody of the upper Red for more than a century. The words of the Chickasaws' franchise "as long as water runs," will continue to be the chief aria of the valley.

— MEN OF MYSTERY —

Glamour is a peculiar thing; it gilds the reputation of some people with such a thick crust that contemporaries can never solve the riddle of its origin, nor can posterity ever break its film of mystery. The Red River Valley has some outstanding examples of glamorized personalities about whom imagination supplies more information than can be gleaned from history or facts. Take the cases of Bean, Stray and Raynal, for examples.

There are a good many people in the valley, and particularly in Bonham, who can retell stories about Tom Bean—his habits, his wealth, his business and above all, the mystery of his family. Mr. Ashley Evans, who was for many years the editor of *The Bonham Favorite,* knew Tom Bean personally, almost intimately. One autumn day in 1940, Mr. Evans recounted some incidents of the man whose home once stood on the spot now occupied by *The Bonham Daily Favorite.* A vivid word-picture of an unusual man was revealed.

Tom Bean appeared in the valley a decade or two before the War Between the States. He liked the lay of the land here, and he knew land and its possibilities. He offered his services as a surveyor to the civil authorities of the state and was eagerly accepted. For his work he was paid in land; there was more of that than there was of money. He settled at Bonham and through a long period of years continued to make the county seat of Fannin his legal residence. From the first there was a dash of glamour about him; he came unaccompanied and he told nothing about himself or his "kin-folks." That in itself was sufficient to prick curiosity. It did.

He was a tall, slender fellow who wore a beegum hat and carried an umbrella. He was quiet but approachable. He was popular even though he was known to dislike all Democrats. He dressed in somewhat better clothes than the men who were felling trees and ploughing around the stumps. Again unlike the majority, he wore no beard.

With their curiosity still unsatisfied, people soon passed upon him the compliment—"he's no scalawag, whatever he is." Numbers of people today voice the same sentiment, almost the same words; they only change the tense form of the verbs. By the more educated he was counted a man of "implicit honesty and absolute integrity" whose judgment was consulted and whose decisions were highly regarded by residents throughout the valley. He seemed to be a man of learning, and they expected him to guide them in matters where technicalities of language and literature were involved.

He was a great lover of books and the "belongings" he brought with him other than his clothes were books. In his little home, which was no larger than a tourist cabin of today, he had shelf upon shelf of books. Something of his character can be seen in his selections, for he was not one to use books for a literary front. His choice fell upon deeds of character; consequently, there were chiefly biographies and dramas upon those shelves. Mr. Bean was evidently an ardent Shakespeare fan for it is said that he knew the Bard of Avon's works "from top to bottom." He was enthusiastic too in his admiration of the new writer, Charles Dickens, whose stories depicted the foibles and perfections of human nature with an uncanny skill. For poetry Mr. Bean cared very little, except as it occurred in the development of Shakespeare's plots.

In answer to the customary salutation—"where you from?" Tom Bean was always evasive. If he were pressed and an answer was demanded he usually said, "Why from a bean patch, of course. Where else would you expect?" But people came to the conclusion that he was from "up North" for he showed familiarity with Washington, D. C., with New York and Virginia.

Tom Bean accumulated land so fast that he did not know its value, nor did he stop to bother with its cultivation. When he needed some money to pay taxes or debts, he rode out and rounded up a bunch of wild horses, brought them in and made settlement, then straightway forgot financial matters until another emergency arose. He owned land in a great many counties, in fact he dipped his finger into every county of Northeast Texas and even into Central and West Texas. One of the best known stories about him is the legend that he made many trips to Austin, on horseback, and could camp on his own land every night. When you consider that it was all of three hundred miles to Austin, that feat of ownership should entitle Tom Bean to be numbered with the plutocracy. A lawyer in Sherman says that Bean owned land in almost every county of the State. In Grayson County alone he owned 25,000 acres. As a matter of comparison the Red River Dam takes a block of 29,000 acres from Grayson County and the task of acquiring that block of 29,000 acres has been regarded as tremendous. But Tom Bean could have made one abstract to almost that entire amount.

 He was a generous person seemingly and made few enemies. When the Cotton Belt railroad was building a spur from Commerce to Sherman, its survey crossed some of Bean's land. Bean immediately donated one hundred acres to the railroad for a townsite. The company returned the compliment by designating a townsite with his name. The village is a creditable marker to this man of mystery.

 Tom Bean's private life was as mysterious as his past and public life. He came in the time of slavery and brought a small retinue of servants with him. The emancipation proclamation made no change in the Bean household; the servants remained in status quo. That very static situation was the cause of many whispered conversations and the motivating force of many lifted eyebrows. It was believed at least by the female population that Tom Bean lived in the modest cabin with a common-law wife and that the young mulattos about the yard were really young Beans. But what could you expect when Mr. Bean always said he had been raised in a bean-patch? If this situation were true—and it *appeared* to be true—the men of the valley ignored it; since it concerned one of their own sex they heartily endorsed the theory that a man's private life was his own.

Although he had never admitted that any relatives of his existed, more than one hundred people came to Bonham and Sherman after his death to file claims for a portion of his estate. That was in the 1880's; Tom Bean had died and been buried in Willow Wild Cemetery at Bonham, thereby running up the public's temperature to fever heat. The excitement of being on the verge of discovery of a long-guarded secret created this acute condition.

The courts tried for a long time to settle the matter. The litigation brought on one of the most famous civil law-suits in Texas history, but the results were vague and complicated. Some claimants were rewarded, others denied, the State got back a lot of its land for non-payment of taxes, and the colored family got only his trunks, clothes and personal effects.

The library he had collected on human character—well who got it? Nobody knows. It disappeared, or probably was carried off as souvenirs by some of the human specimens their owner had loved so well to study. When it was all over, the general public did not know much more about the man who was raised in a bean-patch than it had at the beginning of Bean's residence in the valley.

There was another Fannin County man, John Stray, who was just what his name indicated—a stray. He was a foundling who was adopted by outlaws, and hanged as a horse-thief. The story goes, and it is vouched for by several older residents of Bonham, that some members of the Onstott and McDaniel families found John Stray lying in a ditch by the side of the road as they were returning to their homes near Last Chance. One of the men dismounted and picked up an odd-shaped package which they thought might be whiskey that had been lost by another traveler. When the men saw that it was a baby—and a very young baby—they were so non-plussed and flabbergasted that they had to hold a lengthy conference right there. They decided to take it home with them and later the novel idea of finding a stray baby appealed to them so much that they kept it and brought him up in the way they wanted him to go—contrary to existing laws and against all future laws. They christened him John Stray and made no effort to prove his identity.

Young Stray grew up a credit to his mentors' training. He decided he could surpass them in achievement. He moved farther west and was hanged for a thief in the ranching country near Sweetwater. His life appears a denial of the theory of heredity. Or does it? At any rate he testified for environment.

Just the opposite argument seems to be exemplified in the life of Justin Raynal in Denison, a quiet stranger who spent no more than ten years in Texas and yet clinched his claim to fame. He drifted into the newly-formed railroad town in the Seventies when it was at its wildest and its roughest. He said very little to anybody but he must have liked the place, and have realized its almost complete isolation from all foreign countries except Mexico. And definitely Justin Raynal had had no dealings with the Mexicans or the Spanish for it was obvious that his habits, his accent, and manner were French. There were many drifters in Denison then from "foreign parts." Raynal showed his understanding of this element by setting up soon after his arrival a first-rate saloon on Main Street. Here he featured fine wines and music. It must have been a drinking-spot deluxe. Male Denisonians, one and all, flocked to the place. Raynal made money but he didn't seem to care so much about it. He kept his mouth shut and attended only to his own business.

Judge M. M. Scholl of Denison, recalls that Monsieur Raynal employed an Italian orchestra to furnish music at his saloon and that this new feature did much to increase trade. Thus with Italian operatic music and a Frenchman for bartender, the builders of Denison pursued their merry lives and succeeded at their task besides. The former Snake Editor and several other residents incline to the story that Raynal was a fugitive from justice and found safety in anonymity in a new country. "We sorter thought he'd committed some crime in the old country but he never told it to anyone."

When Raynal died, he left a will. His former customers were surprised to find that he had left all his possessions to the City of Denison for the advancement of its schools. His estate was estimated at $7,000 to $10,000. Denison remembers him — the municipal building stands where he used to feature fine music and fine wine; on a boulevard facing one of the entrances of the Denison High School there is a granite and bronze marker with the name Justin Raynal—nothing more. Unlike the Tom Bean case there were no follow-ups, no claimants, real or phony. The romantics still believe that he was fleeing from a tragic love affair while the bloodthirsty are just as sure that he was running away from murder. It's an unsolved mystery; your guess is as good as the next one.

21

— AUNT MARIA SPEAKS HER MIND —

The misty air of the swamp hung over Jefferson with the heaviness of incense; it came from Little River, Black River, Cypress Bayou and Caddo Lake. It stupefied newcomers and made them think of malaria, quinine and wood fires. There were only a few newcomers there in the Eighties and Nineties and a decade later. Merchants stood on quiet street corners and looked at the deserted wharf or talked about the times when 226 steamboats tied up at that wharf each year, or when 80,000 bales of cotton had been shipped from this small city. They recalled too that one year more than 9,000 bushels of bois d'arc seed had been shipped to distant points.

Sometimes a group of idlers could be seen lingering on the courthouse lawn leaning against the granite statue of the Confederate soldier and talking about the deeds of the soldiers of Jefferson, or the carpetbaggers, or the Federal soldiers who tried to build a stockade in Sand Town. They told some weird stories, too, of Oakwood Cemetery and its Street of Graves where there were hundreds of unmarked graves

—soldiers, bushwhackers, gamblers, babies, wagoners and rivermen.

None knew the past better than did Aunt Maria. There was a weirdness about her that made her a perfect accompaniment to the song of the Bayou. She used to stand for hours on street corners or courthouse steps, gazing with an unseeing eye at the passing figures before her.

She was an ex-slave but the abolition of slavery made very little difference in her way of life. The "white folks" were still her friends; they gave her their cast-off clothes and they gave her "washings," food, and kindling. But there was something queer about her that scared little children and made her the central character of the ghost stories of the young. They said she talked with ghosts in Oakwood Cemetery and that she was liable to come around any dark corner at night time, muttering to herself or to the ghosts that followed her. The young white folks said, "Aunt Maria's goin' t' git cha!" And the young black folks said "Aunt Maria's goin' put a conjur on you!"

Aunt Maria's movements did resemble those of a ghost; that is, they coincided with the old and unrefuted idea of the way a ghost should walk. She never moved rapidly; indeed, she seemed to glide rather than to walk. She wore the old clothing of her white friends, adding, if need be, the one outstanding touch of her personality—floor-length skirts. She trailed her sweeping skirts through dust and mud, through dirt and water. One seldom saw her feet. That's another way in which she resembled the ghosts of our literary and theatrical experience. You have often wondered if these spirits had feet, haven't you? They never seem to use them or need them either in the pictures or the stage sets. Well, that was the way with Aunt Maria; she appeared in unexpected places in Jefferson, mumbling for an hour or more to her unseen listener. One night I followed her to the Street of Graves.

It was just after sunset of a summer evening. The dust was deep in the streets and sounds of crickets and bullfrogs filled the air with lonesomeness. "Aunt Maria, Aunt Maria," I called, but received no answer. That gliding, dusty skirt swept on. I had often heard the story of how Aunt Maria would wander through Oakwood and hold conversations at each tombstone or wooden cross. That evening I had a mind to follow her and listen to those words.

"Mis' comin' up; mis' comin' up f'um de lake. Spirits goin' walk dis night; spirits goin' walk on de lake. Yes suh, I sees 'em. Who dat in front? Who dat?"

"Yes, who *is* that, Aunt Maria?" I asked as I endeavored to catch up with her. We were approaching the gates of the cemetery not the lake, but her vision, so it seemed, extended to Caddo Lake.

"Dat's de Senator, dat's who tis. I dun seen 'im walkin' out dere befo'. He goin' walk a'gin at midnight and at break o' day. He lookin' fuh someone; he got his gun, yes sir, he got his pistol."

She glided farther from me; I stumbled over fallen stones and cave-ins on the Street of Graves as I followed. As yet I was not alarmed, nor ready to quit my quest of the curious, if not the supernatural. I knew the story about which Aunt Maria was talking; it was one of the famous murder cases of the early Republic.

The Senator was Senator Robert Potter whose home was on a bluff overlooking the lake. He was said to have been on friendly if not intimate terms with President Lamar, and to have shown partiality in the granting of political favors. For this he aroused the enmity of the "Lion of the Lakes," otherwise Captain William Pickney Rose who also had a home on Caddo Lake. The Senator's home was known as "Potter's Point."

Each tried to ensnare the other in a plot of trespass. The Senator violated the terms of trespass on Rose's land and in turn Rose and his followers organized a posse and surrounded Potter's Point. From midnight till dawn they kept watch and when one of the Senator's slaves appeared they fired upon him with buckshot. The Senator realizing he was trapped made a break for the lake about one hundred yards away. He was an expert diver and swimmer and his plunge into the lake and his disappearance from sight were not unexpected by the posse who were close upon his heels. Consequently when the Senator came up for air after what had seemed sufficient time to fool any posse, he was spotted immediately by the watching possemen on the bank and was instantly killed by one of them. Then they pulled his body out and there was a friendly burial at Potter's Point. The career of the fiery South Carolinian was finished in 1843, but people used to say—and those people included both white and colored—that the Senator walked through the mists of the marshes and the lake still seeking revenge upon his enemies. Hence, it couldn't be the Senator's spirit Aunt Maria was pursuing for he did not frequent Oakwood.

"Aunt Maria, Aunt Maria! Where are you?" Darkness had set in and I could not distinguish her among the monuments of former Jeffersonians. I stopped quite still to listen. Then I heard her voice mumbling, "Heah you is, heah you is." I felt my way to the nearest pine tree and leaned against it with a feeling of security. I thought that if I could touch something alive I could give better attention to Aunt Maria's conversation.

"You dun broke yo' chains, ain' cha? I ain' su'prised. I wuz dere dat day; I seen yuh fightin'. I knowed yuh wuz goin' git killed. Yes suh. Ain't no good fuh two men to love one woman. Somebody goin' git hu't fuh sho. Missuh Rober'son, yuh an' Missuh Rose wouldn' b'leeve dat. You jis had t' go on an' shoot it out. An' heah you is. An' you ain' been restin' easy since yuh dun it, has yuh? De white folks, dey put yuh heah wid dese two iron posts chained t'gether so as t' hol' yuh down dere. Hit didn' do no good tho'. Heah's yo' chains all broke, like yuh dun busted out. I tol' 'em—all dem white folks—dat you'd do dat case yuh wuz tryin' t' make peace wid yo' soul. I been tellin' 'em dat yuh wuz walkin'. H'mn, yuh didn' git yo' posts back in neider; dey's all loose. Yuh ain' goin' git no peace, white man, tell yuh gits dat blood off yo' han's. No suh, ol' Maria knows what she knows; God tells huh 'bou t'ings."

The voice drifted, the figure moved. I detached myself from the pine tree and called in what seemed to me a very loud voice. "Aunt Maria, where are you going now?" The moving figure took no notice of my question.

"I got t' go ovah heah an' talk t' dis po' chile. Di'mons don' do nobody no good, no suh, dey don'." I knew now where she was going—to the grave of Diamond Bessie. The story of poor Bessie and her diamonds was familiar to every resident of North Texas. Her murder brought on one of the big legal battles of Texas history—seven years of litigation and an acquittal on a technicality for her husband who had been twice sentenced to death. Bessie's grave in Oakwood had been visited by hundreds, and many fantastic and unbelievable stories were told of the beautiful young girl who spent only three days in Jefferson. She wore diamonds, so many that she was gaudy; she wore fine clothes, so fine that she was conspicuous. Her husband, too, was flashy. They said they were from the North, the East, or some other unknown region.

"Dis po' chile, she wa'nt t' blame. Dat bad man jus' 'ticed her off wid dem di'mon's. He wuz jus' a scalawag an' oughta' been hung. Dat wuz a mean white man an' treat dis' perty lil' gal wrong. I'll bring yuh flow'rs, Miss Bessie, jus' as soon as I kin git some. Ol' Maria don' forgit yuh wuz nice to her dat time at de hotel. Yuh jus' wait, Miss Bessie, dese heah folks ain' goin' t' forgit yuh. Stay still, chile; 'twon't do yuh no good t' walk."

Having given this advice to the unquiet Bessie she turned and glided out of the cemetery and turned her steps toward town. Although I *heard* automobile sirens and saw electric and neon signs I followed this spectre of the past in fascination. I thought she might hesitate at the Excelsior Hotel, she knew so many stories that had happened there. And she did stop on the corner across the street from the old hotel with its veranda of iron-grille trimmings and its aviary of singing canaries.

"Who dat man say he goin' rune us folks heah? How come he say he kin do dat? G'wan, Missuh Goul', you ain' got nothin' but a railroad. Us folks in Jefferson ain' skeered of yuh. De boats goin' come back heah some day. Yes suh, ol' Maria knows."

She shook her fist at the hotel before she moved on, the gesture seemingly in retaliation of Jay Gould's threat that Jefferson would rue the day it snubbed his offer of a railroad. I had just about reached the stage now where I had begun to think that Aunt Maria did know what she was talking about. Water navigation for Jefferson was not dead. Some day we would hear again the clear call of the boat whistles.

When I caught up with Aunt Maria again she was at the Methodist Church with her gaze fixed upon the belfry tower. She turned rather quickly and swept right by me, but as she passed I heard her say, "I'm goin' tell Missuh Sedberry an' Missuh Taylor 'bout dis, yes I is. Ol' Maria knows."

I turned and looked back at the church but I could see nothing wrong. I half-expected to see ghosts gliding from the tower or find that the great silver bell had fallen. Perhaps Aunt Maria was hastening to spread the news of disaster, but no, nothing had changed. Then perhaps she wanted to tell her story of the bell to the editor of the *Jimplecute,* that friend of the people since 1865. This little journal had told in print several times the legend of the silver bell.

In 1854 the Methodists of Jefferson had wanted a beautiful bell for their church; a silver bell was none too good they said. They wanted the clear metallic ring of silver on silver such as they heard when they clicked dollar upon dollar. So, they took up a collection of silver dollars, but Mexican silver dollars, 1500 of them. They sent the money to an Eastern foundry and when the bell was returned it gave universal satisfaction and peace to the hearts and ears of the Methodists.

In my dilatory gazing at the church I had lost Aunt Maria from view. Like the ghosts she communed with she had a habit of disappearing suddenly and quietly. I continued my way to Sedberry's Drug Store. She was not there but I did not mind.

I had enough of my visit to the Street of Graves with Aunt Maria's ghostly comments. There were people here, so many people, live people, well-known people, lovable people! Sedberry's—the Heart of Jefferson! Apothecaries for the ailing since 1865 and never a change in the name or ownership of the store! Medicine-mixers who knew their business, your business, the town's business, the world's business! I dropped contentedly upon a stool to listen.

* * * * * *

'Twas just a dream I had: A dream of Jefferson! I had been reading too much history; I suffered a reaction—a pleasing, hypnotic reaction. However, in the light of day and sensibility I still believe that Aunt Maria was right. She did know; those boats will come back to Jefferson some day. What's one railroad? Driftwood! Driftwood!

22

— Remembrance —

Three gentlemen made a hurried departure from Washington-on-the-Brazos in the spring of 1836. There was so much excitement after the signing of Texas' Declaration of Independence that friend became separated from friend.

Mr. Richard Ellis, Mr. Collin McKinney and Mr. Albert Latimer had represented the Red River district at the convention and had planned the return trip together. But in some manner Mr. Latimer became lost from his friends and set out alone, traveling mule-back to Red River and thinking he might overtake them en route.

The new-born republic was scantily furnished with trails, highways or markers, and in Mr. Latimer's anxiety to overtake his friends he missed the beaten trail altogether. One evening at dusk as he rounded a thicket of oak trees his mule stumbled into an Indian village. He knew instantly that the Indians were unfriendly when he saw them rush from their teepees with spears. Mr. Latimer was a young man of twenty-eight and accustomed to the ways of pioneer life but he knew then that he and his mule had made a big mistake. They were not welcome here and they could not get away. He showed the predilection for logic and reason that later in life advanced him to judgeship after judgeship. The young Mr. Latimer probably did not realize his motive, but he was cornered and he knew it. So, he just sat still on his mule.

Suddenly an Indian appeared in the doorway of a teepee, raised his hand and said "How." He was a tall brave Indian, and Mr. Latimer regarded him with interest. It was his only hope.

The Indian advanced in a friendly manner. Then Mr. Latimer recognized him. He had seen him several times in Clarksville and had befriended him on two occasions when he had been falsely accused by white settlers of the community.

The Indian took Mr. Latimer to his teepee and that night slept just outside it to guard the safety of his guest. The next morning he gave him some parched corn and dried venison to take with him for the remainder of his trip. Furthermore, he rode with him until high noon to be sure that he set him on the right trail north.

Mr. Latimer reached Clarksville, his home, in safety and in gratitude. Truly, an Indian never forgets.

23

— Lost Colleges —

COPY OF AN ADVERTISEMENT
INSERTED
IN THE
COLUMNS OF THE PRESENT
WITH
AN APPEAL FOR A REPRINT IN
THE
COLUMNS OF THE FUTURE

LOST—Sometime between 1860 and 1920 ten colleges which disseminated culture in the Red River Valley. Each is known to have been on intimate terms with Distress and Poverty prior to his disappearance. When last seen each was dressed in very shabby clothes and was endeavoring to make his way to Prosperity by way of Pride.

Three of the missing colleges were trim, petite and appealing; three were sturdy and militaristic, and three were everyday and sensible. Four made their homes in Sherman (once called the Athens of North Texas), three made their headquarters in very small villages in order to be close to the rural scene, and three dwelt in medium-sized towns of the valley. All of them were known and loved by thousands.

Anyone knowing the whereabouts of these absconded culture containers is requested to notify Texas History, telephone 1945, State Archives, Austin, Texas. In view of the present bewilderment it is considered that Urgent Necessity may have to recall missing leaders of educational sects to quiz them upon how people reacted when they pursued higher learnings in past eras. The names of the ten are listed below:

MARY NASH, Sherman
KIDD-KEY, Sherman
CARR-BURDETTE, Sherman
LETELLIER'S, Sherman
SAVOY, Savoy
MACKENZIE'S, Clarksville
GRAYSON, Whitewright
PARIS FEMALE SEMINARY, Paris
COLUMBIA, Van Alstyne
CARLTON, Bonham

24

— Sidelight on a Robber —

Jesse James knew the Red River Valley well; he liked it and visited it many times. Grayson County was one of his favorite haunts. He rode its trails and visited its towns peaceably, sociably and forcibly. But there is one story about him that shows a different side of his nature. It took place at Pilot Grove, that point in the southeastern corner of the county often called Lick Skillet and sometimes Four Corners.

In the days when the Military, the Lees, Peacocks and others were fighting it out, Jesse James rode up to a farmhouse one day and called a loud "hello." He was riding a spirited horse, and a six-year-old girl sat in the saddle with him. She waved her hand at the woman who opened the front door a crack.

The little girl's gesture gave the woman courage to walk out to the gate. Those were the days when a person couldn't be too careful, but the woman figured that such a pretty little girl couldn't be riding with a thief or a robber or a feudist. She ventured to the gate and spoke: "Howdy! What's for you?"

"I'm Jesse James, Ma'am, but don't be skeered. I jus' want t' leave this little girl here with you for a spell. I'll be back through here in about six weeks. It's so I can't take her with me. Oh, you'll be paid for it and paid well."

"But I got my own children to look after and I ain't got time to see after any more."

Jesse James took a pistol from his belt. "Oh yes, you have, Ma'am."

"Well, she *is* a mighty perty little thing. Is she sickly or bad?"

"She'll give you no trouble, Ma'am. Jus' you take her in now an' say nothin' to nobody 'bout it. An' you need'n' be uneasy. I'll be back an' bring you your money. Down you go, Becky."

The farm-woman took the pretty little Becky in the house, for Jesse was gone as suddenly as he had come. In the weeks that followed she kept her mouth shut and she stayed at home. Few people heard about her boarder. Becky gave her no trouble, just as Jesse had promised. She was such an agreeable little girl that she earned a welcome from the other children of the home. She was imaginative and passed on her new games and ideas to the children who followed her lead most willingly.

About three weeks after Jesse had deposited Becky at this secluded farm home, a squad of the Military rode up to the gate. The officers quizzed the woman about Jesse James. They told her that he had been in the neighborhood recently, and that they were on his trail to arrest him. The woman steadily answered "no" to all questions.

"I ain't seen nothin' of 'im; don't know nothin' 'bout 'im."

Little Becky smiled sweetly at the officers when they left. She hadn't said a word. She was busy playing with six other children.

In six weeks Jesse James returned to the farm-house for the child. He not only paid the woman what he had promised but double the amount. He took Becky and rode away and that was the last the woman saw of him, really and truly that time.

Who was little Becky? Nobody ever knew. Was she hostage, daughter or friend? Whoever she was, she seemed to hold Jesse's affection and esteem. Mark it "Credit" on Jesse's account.

25

— THE SNAKE EDITOR SPEAKS —

Have you ever met the Snake Editor? No? Then come with me; perhaps we can catch him at his office. He's one of the most individual characters in our valley and his projects and activities are indissolubly blended with those of Denison, the "Gate City" (one of them) of Texas. First we must climb this long flight of stairs to his office; the steps are wooden ones and dirty, and there's a deep depression in the center of each one, footprints of time that will throw you off balance if you fail to hit the same mark. But think nothing of it; it's the same flight of steps that the Editor has been climbing for over fifty years.

Here's his office. There's a little tin sign hanging outside the green door which says—"Justice of the Peace"—but that's right. The Snake Editor is now a justice of the peace. Just open the green door and go on in. There may be some legal or corporate matter going on but never mind. Everything is quite informal here. It is a spring morning and the windows are open. Two huge desks of the style of several decades ago are beside the windows which face Main Street. Justice Wright and Justice Scholl preside here, but the Snake Editor's desk is the one on the raised platform with the high-backed swivel chair behind it. We're lucky, for there he is in it. There's a jaunty look about him too, that indicates he's fit to be interviewed.

He's a tall, slender gentleman, and he wears a very neat and also new gray suit. He's abreast of the season and knows it, for he wears a sprig of plum blossom in the lapel of his coat. They say he always wears a flower in his buttonhole. Note too that the deep blue of his tie matches the clear blue of his eyes. His hair, and there's plenty of it yet, is as white as the infrequent snows which fall in Denison. But what are you looking at so intently? His "side-burns"? It's been many a day since you've seen such side whiskers as these—long flowing tufts of hair growing down from his ears. They might be braided, curled, or cut but the Snake Editor wears them loose and flowing. He can spin yarns by the hour. Go ahead and ask him.

"Experiences? Say, listen, talk about Tom Sawyer—that's nothing to what's happened in my life. When I was a baby in Clay County, Missouri, I ran off a band of robbers because I made such a racket they couldn't stand it. It's a fact; Quantrell and his men rode away in disgust because they couldn't work in such noise. Good thing I made such a hullabaloo for all the time my mother was wearing $2,000 in a buckskin belt underneath her home-spun dress.

"Our family always liked to untie hard knots. My great-grandfather was Daniel Boone and my father was a Forty-niner. Nothing but natural when I got grown, or thought I was, that I should want to see new country, so I pushed on a little farther west than Missouri. I came to Texas. I didn't get any farther than right here, just over the Red River; didn't need to; found plenty o' hard knots and pretty soon I pitched into 'em.

"I landed here in the late Seventies. I remember that I wore a hand-tailored Scotch-plaid suit and that I was a pretty scrawny, sorry sapling. Fact of the business, the Doctor in Missouri said I had consumption and wasn't fit to travel. I decided to cure myself. There were lots of Indians around here then and when I watched them riding and the cowboys rounding up cattle, I thought I saw a way to do it. I managed to trade for a shotgun, a saddle horse and a fishing pole and I lived two years with the cowboys and the Indians, always in the open. That did the trick. I'm still here and my folks I had back there, the whole durned outfit, are out in the cemetery. Yes sir, that life in the open is the reason the old Snake Editor is here today.

"My name then? Pshaw, I ran around here for more'n fifty years without any name but Snake Editor an' they called me that all the way from San Antonio to St. Louis. It come about like this.

"When I got here I already knew something about printing, because I'd been bound out for five years to a printer at fifty cents a month.

After I had got myself cured, I was ready to go to work. I started right in working for an uncle of mine. He established a paper—*The Denison Dispatch*—and there's where the Snake Editor got his start. I had a column; must have been one of the first columnists in North Texas. But I'll tell you, we were building an empire and I saw and heard things I had to speak about. People came here from everywhere. There was a story that we had some ex-pirates in here and that piratical gold was helping build the new town. I don't know about that but we got the town built and we've done a good job.

"I learned to be a world traveler by just sitting at home and listening to these men from everywhere, all working for the same purpose —to found a great Southwest Empire here. I talked to the Chinese about China; learned about Arabia from the Arabs, Russia from the Russians, and so on and on. Of course we had a good many English, French, Italians and Germans. We had plenty of music and entertainments; buffalo hunting was the common sport, gambling was popular, and saloons were flourishing. We had thirty-five saloons on Main Street at one time.

"The Epstein Bar was the most famous of all the saloons. It was a private bar and every man was asked to carve his initials there. Some of the most famous men of the country inscribed their initials at the Epstein.

"I began agitatin' for a bridge to take the place of Colbert's Ferry. I kept that up, and

THE SNAKE EDITOR SPEAKS

finally we had a toll bridge. I made myself unpopular with some but there were plenty of others who were backing me up. Frank Colbert owned the franchise, and the Bridge Company had to settle with him. Well, we finally got the bridge up and it cost you ten cents to walk across it to Indian Territory. Then the river come along and washed the bridge away three years after it was built, but by and by we got another one. Still, the old Snake Editor wasn't satisfied.

"I begun agitatin' for a *free* bridge. That did stir up a furore. Some of the Bridge people come and threatened to blow my head off if I didn't keep my mouth shut about a free bridge. That did me good and I laughed in their faces and agitated worse than ever. Well, things moved along and in 1931 we got the free bridge. Oh, I'm a newspaper man first to last and a firm believer in the power of the press. This little ol' Justice business here—well, I've been fooling with it some time too but what I'm proudest of is that we really made that Southwest Empire here in Texas. Excuse me a minute, I got to see what this woman wants."

He's out of his swivel chair like a flash and down to the cherry-wood railing where a colored woman waits to tell her troubles to the Judge. The interview's over; might as well go down to the street again. The Judge is still looking for hard knots to untie and stories to unwind. He's busy with the present and he'll talk no more about the past this day. There's one thing certain to remember—as long as the Judge is around here he'll be "agitatin'" for something.

Is the Snake Editor still running around without a name? Well, hardly; he's M. M. Scholl, native of Missouri, builder of the Red River Valley, exponent of the freedom of the press and at present Justice of the Peace in the city of Denison.

When the Railroads Came to the Valley

The 1870's mark the advance of the railroads. They changed the map of the valley because towns were abandoned, established, changed and moved. There was a frantic rush to follow the shining rails, to settle along their right-of-way just as earlier there had been a rush to follow the river's course. Towns sprang up and disappeared like magic.

Note a few changes wrought at the beginning of the era. Texarkana, the state-line city, came into prominence; Jefferson shrank away for snubbing its nose at Capital's scheme. Sherman stood pat and lost the "Katy's" entrance into Texas thereby. Denison (that just missed being called Red River City) came into power and has shared with Sherman, fifty-fifty, ever since. Gainesville lost its standing as a cattle center to Fort Worth and Wichita Falls. Paris forged ahead of Bonham and Clarksville—the last two named maintained their peaceful unobtrusiveness.

Most of the buildings in Kentucky Town were put on wheels and pulled three miles to join Whitewright on the tracks of the Katy. The settlement of White Mound did likewise to join Tom Bean beside the Cotton Belt. Preston Bend, Doan's Store and Red River Station became ghost towns. Dallas became the great city. Many people of Grayson County say that if Sherman had been alert to the opportunities offered by the railroads it would have been the big city of North Texas rather than Dallas. Many newcomers at that time looked both of them over and selected Sherman as the coming metropolis.

Cattle trails grew up in weeds and the cowboy drifted farther west. Industry and the Machine Age staked their claims. The first era in the valley was finished and the second set in to prepare the way for the third—super paved highways, super motor buses and trucks, super factories, super electric power from super dams, and super plane service for the residents of our valley.

BIBLIOGRAPHY

BIBLIOGRAPHY

Printed Matter

Down the Texas Road, Grant Foreman, University of Oklahoma Press, 1936.
The Northern Standard. Files 1858-1860-1861-1862-1865.
The Bonham Favorite. Special Historical Edition, July 22, 1940.
The Gainesville Register. 50th Anniversary Edition, Sept. 23, 1940.
The Sherman Democrat. 60th Anniversary Edition, Aug. 13, 1939.
The History of Lamar County, A. W. Neville, North Texas Publishing Company, Paris, Texas, 1937.
A History of Grayson County, Texas, Mattie Davis Lucas and Mita Holsapple Hall, Scruggs Publishing Company, Sherman, Texas, 1936.
History of Fannin County, Carter.
History of Oklahoma, Jos. B. Thoburn and Isaac M. Holcomb, Daub and Company, San Francisco, California, 1908.
Adventures on Red River, Capt. R. B. Marcy, University of Oklahoma Press, 1937.
History of Cooke County. Mss. and papers of Miss Lillian Gunter, Library of Department of History, North Texas State Teachers College, Denton.
History of Cooke County. Booklet, "Ye Gainesville Towne," compiled by Junior High School, 1927.
A History of Jefferson. Compiled by Mrs. Arch McKay and Mrs. H. A. Spellings, from various newspapers, 1936.
History of Red River County, Clark.
A Pictorial History of Texas, H. S. Thrall, N. D. Thompson & Co., St. Louis, 1879.
Reconstruction in Texas, C. W. Ramsdell.
"History of Lee-Peacock Feud," T. U. Taylor in *Leonard Graphic,* 1940.
A Short History of Denison, Jack Maguire, 1938.

BIBLIOGRAPHY

The Denison Guide, American Guide Series, compiled by Federal Writers' Project of WPA, in Texas, 1939, published by Chamber of Commerce.

Interviews

Mr. J. H. Whitsett
Mr. J. P. Darwin
Mr. Daniel Jackson
Mrs. D. B. Holman
Mrs. I. Beasley
Mr. F. E. Vittitoe
Mr. James Breckeen
Miss Mary M. Clark
Mrs. H. L. Pierson
Mr. J. D. Hoard
Mrs. Wade Parks
Judge M. M. Scholl
Mr. Ashley Evans

Mr. Bryan Weber
Mrs. Kate L. Kincaid
Mr. Eddie Binion
Mr. Tom Holmes
Mr. Lee Hampton
Mrs. Pearl Connelly
Mr. R. W. Ball
Mr. Roy Neathery
Miss Maude Collins
Mr. E. V. Bowers
Mrs. Amanda Butler (colored)